Thinking for a Living

"WILSON, WHAT EXACTLY IS A
KNOWLEDGE WORKER AND DO
WE HAVE ANY ON THE STAFF?"

Thinking for a Living

How to Get Better
Performance and
Results from
Knowledge Workers

Thomas H. Davenport

Harvard Business School Press
Boston, Massachusetts

Library of Congress Cataloging-in-Publication Data

Davenport, Thomas H., 1954–
    Thinking for a living : how to get better performance and results from knowledge
workers / Thomas H. Davenport.
        p.   cm.
    Includes index.
    ISBN 1-59139-423-6
    1. Knowledge workers. 2. Knowledge management. 3. Intellectual capital. I. Title.
HD8039.K59D38 2005
658.3—dc22

                                                                        2005002390

The paper used in this publication meets the minimum requirements of the American
National Standard for Information Sciences—Permanence of Paper for Printed Library
Materials, ANSI Z39.48-1992.

Contents

Preface and Acknowledgments

I've been planning this book for a long time, and it goes deeply into my intellectual interests and background. It's at the intersection of two areas in which I've done a lot of work: processes and knowledge. In the late 1980s I started to research the improvement and management of business processes. By 1993 or so I had realized that to address knowledge-intensive processes required a different set of approaches than most companies were using for process reengineering and improvement. Then, around 1994, I started researching and writing about knowledge management. For several years I argued that knowledge management ought to involve "people, process, and technology," but I didn't pay much attention to the process side of this combo until the late 1990s.

Because I knew that I would eventually write this book, I undertook a series of studies involving knowledge workers and their work that I hoped would become key building blocks or chapters. Most of these involved collaborators, and I'd like to thank them now for their help with these research projects and the ideas that resulted from them. The first was undertaken with Sirkka Jarvenpaa of the University of Texas and Mike Beers, then of Ernst & Young. It resulted in a 1996 *Sloan Management Review* article called "Improving Knowledge Work Processes," and many of its concepts can be found in chapters 2 and 4.

I became the Director of the Accenture Institute for Strategic Change in 1998, and I worked with several colleagues there on projects that made their way into this book in some form. The matrix of four knowledge work types that I use here came from a project on knowledge management that I worked on a bit with Jeanne Harris and Leigh Donoghue. Then Bob Thomas, Sue Cantrell, and I collaborated on a project we called "The Art of Work: Improving the Performance of High-End Knowledge Workers." It led to most of the ideas in chapter 8 of this book. Sue and I also worked with Rob Cross of the University of Virginia on a project assessing the social networks of high-performing knowledge workers; this research formed the basis of chapter 7. Chapter 9 is the result of an attempt at coauthoring an article with Warren Bennis on the management and leadership of knowledge workers. It never really emerged as a coauthored piece, but I was happy to use the ideas Warren and I had discussed as the basis for a talk at his Festschrift celebration and a chapter in his Festschrift volume.

While still at Accenture, I was able to begin working with a consortium of IT firms called the Information Work Productivity Council (IWPC). Microsoft started the ball rolling, and Accenture, Cisco, Hewlett-Packard, Intel, SAP, and Xerox also got behind it. When I left Accenture for Babson in 2003, I became the Academic Director of this consortium, and also led a particular research project on "Personal Information and Knowledge Management" that became the core of chapter 6. On the IWPC project I worked closely with Susan Conway of Microsoft, Dan Holtshouse of Xerox, Mary Lee Kennedy (then of Microsoft), and Carla O'Dell of the American Productivity and Quality Center.

Since coming to Babson, I've worked on a couple of projects related to this book within the Working Knowledge Research Center and the Process Management Research Center. There are about forty sponsors of these two programs, so I can't name them all. But I'm grateful to the managers who joined me in exploring issues around "High-Performing Knowledge Worker Environments" and "Managing Knowledge-Intensive Processes." Brad Power, the Executive Director of the Process Management program, gave me much useful feedback on my ideas, and Larry

Prusak, codirector of the Working Knowledge program, has been a source of insights, inspirations, and lively gossip for more than a decade.

I make my living writing the stories of adventurous businesspeople, and this book is no exception. I'd like to thank all the managers who donated their experiences for me to package up into these pages. There are many of them, but John Glaser at Partners Health Care, Kevin Adams at BT, and Luke Koons of Intel are both typical and exemplary.

I've had a great relationship with Harvard Business School Press for more than a decade, and I still think they are the classiest act among business publishers. Melinda Merino was a great editor who never failed to stimulate more and better authorial thinking with her informal and formal comments. I also got very helpful comments from four anonymous reviewers, although I deduced that two of them were Dan Holtshouse and Sue Cantrell, so I can thank them by name. I'd also like to thank Hollis Heimbouch for long-lasting support, Monica Jainschigg for skilled copy editing, Marcy Barnes-Henrie for seeing this book through production, and Zeenat Potia and her team for an appealing cover design.

My wife Jodi continues to help with my work as agent, adviser, reader, friend, and lover. I couldn't have written this or any other book without her. My wonderful sons Hayes and Chase remain largely oblivious to their dad's books, but I write them in part because I hope that someday they'll be proud of them. Bucky, my favorite dog of all time, died during the creation of this book, and I will miss having him at my feet as I write.

1

What's a Knowledge
Worker, Anyway?

Robin feels out of control. She's the head of press and analyst relations for a large professional services firm. Eight people report to her, all of them knowledge workers. Some deal with particular types of press relationships, others with technology industry analysts. She manages some relationships herself. Her job is to improve her company's image with these external audiences—even to her, a somewhat vague and difficult-to-measure mission.

Only half of the people on her staff are with her at headquarters in New York, and only one of the four in New York are on her floor. They're all pretty independent in their work habits, and she doesn't see most of them very often. Several of them frequently work from home. The team used to try to get together monthly, but the company has put restrictions on travel budgets, so they can't do that anymore. Robin feels that much of the time she doesn't know exactly what her people are doing. Sure, she hears about meetings they're having in their weekly conference call, but what are they doing when they're not having a few meetings? She thinks she trusts them, but always has nagging doubts about how hard and how effectively they're working.

She's put some measures in place for her group, such as numbers of media mentions or favorable ratings in analysts' reports. But when things don't go well, her people always have a ready explanation—"One of our strongest thought leaders left the practice," or "That analyst has always had a grudge against us." But how else can she assess the strength of such intangible qualities as "relationships" or "image"? And in many cases, her people are right—they have closer relationships with the reporters, editors, and analysts they deal with than Robin does. She knows the business well from having done it herself, but she also realizes that the job varies a lot from day to day and is highly dependent on interpersonal factors. As a result, she's reluctant to criticize what seems like poor performance too directly; she can't afford to lose the relationships and insights her people have built up over time.

Some of her analysts are definitely more productive than others, however. One, for example, generates twice the press coverage and meets with twice as many industry analysts as anyone else in the group. Other analysts in the group discount her performance—"The service lines she represents just have more to say than mine do"—but Robin thinks it's something this analyst does. Robin has tried to figure out the secret to her success, but has never directly discussed it with her. She's afraid that the high-performing analyst will ask for a raise if she addresses her sterling performance too directly.

Robin is always trying to think of ways to get more out of her team members, but is rarely convinced she's found the answer. On this week's conference call, for example, she plans to announce an initiative to communicate her firm's new marketing campaign to the press and analysts. She's sure that some of her more vocal team members will remind her that "the channel is already overloaded; we can't push more through it." In fact, the situation is worse than they suspect; she's been told by her boss that she may have to lay off one employee due to a budget cut for next year. Everyone will have to do more with less; everyone needs to be more productive. But Robin finds it difficult to imagine how she can get more results from people whom she rarely sees, and who know their jobs better than she does. In the short run, she decides to just call a reporter she's been trying to build a relationship with—it's easier to do her own knowledge work than to improve that of others.

Like Robin, you and I—and most of our friends and colleagues—are knowledge workers. We all think for a living. Like Robin, many of us manage other knowledge workers. We're all doing our work the best we can—or are we? Can we, like Robin, figure out a way to get better results from knowledge workers? Most of us have never even analyzed our own performance, or had much help from our employers in making us more productive and effective. We want to become more efficient at doing our jobs—and to help others do so as well—but we just don't know how. We know more about our own work than just about anyone else, so it's hard for a manager to improve our performance—and in any case we don't like to be told what to do. We've never thought about the fact that we are knowledge workers, or about the implications of that fact for how we carry out and improve our daily activities. What difference does it make that we are knowledge workers? It's certainly not a new thing. This category of work has existed for centuries—think about medieval monks, or the first professors at universities—so why write about them now? Well, as I'll argue a little later in this chapter, if nothing else they're important because they are a large category of workers—probably larger than ever before as a percentage of the workforce in sophisticated economies.

But regardless of the size of this category of workers, it's a very important one. Knowledge workers are responsible for sparking innovation and growth in your organization. They invent your new products and services, design your marketing programs, and create your strategies. In the current economy, they are the horses that pull the plow of economic progress. If our companies are going to be more profitable, if our strategies are going to be successful, if our society is going to become more advanced—it will be because knowledge workers did their work in a more productive and effective manner.

The Growing Importance of Knowledge Workers

Of course, the rise of knowledge work has been foreseen for many years.[1]Automation in factories and farms more than a century ago freed most of the workforce from having to perform physical labor. Over the last half-century, the advent of computers and the pervasive presence of information created a demand for workers who could produce the information in the first place, extract meaning from it, and take action on it. The economist Fritz Machlup did much of the early spadework on knowledge and knowledge work roles; as early as 1958 he stated that knowledge workers comprised almost a third of the U.S. workforce, and that the knowledge work sector was growing twice as fast as the rest of the economy.[2]

In the early twenty-first century, it's likely that a quarter to a half of workers in advanced economies are knowledge workers whose primary tasks involve the manipulation of knowledge and information (see "How Many Are There?"). Even if they're not a majority of all workers, they have the most influence on their economies. They are paid the most, they add the most economic value, and they are the greatest determinant of the worth of their companies. Companies with a high proportion of knowledge workers—let's call them knowledge-intensive—are the fastest-growing and most successful in the United States and other leading economies, and have generated most of these economies' growth in the past couple of decades. The market value of many knowledge-intensive companies—which includes the market's perception of the value of knowledge and knowledge workers—dwarfs their book values, which includes only tangible assets (and the ratio of market to book value in U.S. companies has doubled over the past twenty years, suggesting a great acceleration of knowledge asset value). Even in so-called "industrial" companies, knowledge is increasingly used to differentiate physical goods and to fuel diversification into product-related services. As James Brian Quinn has pointed out, high proportions of workers in manufacturing firms (roughly 90 percent in semiconductors, for example) never touch the manufacturing process, but instead provide knowledge-based services such as marketing, distribution, or customer service.[3]

It's already apparent that the firms with the highest degree and quality of knowledge work tend to be the fastest-growing and most profitable. Microsoft, for example, is one of the most profitable organizations in the history of the planet. Pharmaceutical firms not only produce sophisticated and life-saving drug treatments, they also tend to have high profit margins. Growth industries generally tend to be those with a high proportion of knowledge workers.

How Many Are There?

GIVEN THE IMPRECISE definitions in the world of knowledge work and knowledge workers, it's impossible to specify just how many there are in any particular country. But there are many knowledge workers in advanced economies such as the United States and Europe, no matter how they are defined. At a minimum they comprise a quarter of the U.S. workforce, and at maximum about half.

The U.S. Bureau of Labor Statistics (BLS) doesn't classify knowledge workers, but it puts U.S. workers into categories that can be (somewhat arbitrarily, to be sure) defined as either knowledge workers or not. I would put the following categories into the knowledge worker camp:

- Management
- Business and financial operations
- Computer and mathematical
- Architecture and engineering
- Life, physical, and social scientists
- Legal
- Healthcare practitioners
- Community and social services
- Education, training, and library
- Arts, design, entertainment, sports, media

The classification above yields about 36 million knowledge workers in the United States alone, or 28 percent of the labor force. While no classification scheme is perfect (for example, professional athletes are included in the knowledge worker group, because the U.S. government data lumps them in with arts, design, entertainment, and media workers), it's clear that most people in these jobs think for a living.

Using somewhat less conservative classification criteria than mine (they include clerical workers, for example), Rubin and Huber concluded that there were about 45 million knowledge workers in 1980.[a] Perhaps the simplest measure is the BLS category of "managerial, professional, and technical" workers, which was about 34 percent of the workforce in 2003. Another approach to determining the number of knowledge workers focuses on the percentage of the workforce that actually possesses the skills to do knowledge work. A U.S. Department of Education report suggests that about 25 percent of U.S. workers have the ability to process complex or moderately complex information in mathematical or verbal form, and turn it into knowledge. Using yet another set of criteria to define "information workers" (every approach has its peculiarities—in this case, for example, the category includes 50 percent of "hucksters"), Marc Porat calculated in 1977 that these workers comprised about half of the workforce, and that their total compensation passed that of non–information workers at about that time.[b]

Countries other than the United States, of course, have different definitions of knowledge workers and different numbers, although they are in the same ballpark. Statistics Canada, for example, defines knowledge workers as including management, professional, and technical occupations, and concludes that these comprised 25 percent of the Canadian workforce in 2001 (up from 14 percent in 1971).[c] A study of over 28 million jobs in the United Kingdom found that 32 percent were knowledge-based, requiring a college degree.[d]

There is also some evidence that knowledge workers will continue to be important from a purely numerical standpoint. In the United States, for example, the BLS projects that ten specific occupations will be the fastest-growing in the current decade. At least three of these ten—registered nurses, computer support specialists, and IT software engineers—are pretty clearly knowledge workers, and they all fall into the top half of hourly earnings in the U.S. economy. This suggests that the quarter-to-a-third proportion of knowledge workers in sophisticated economies will persist or grow over time.

a. Michael R. Rubin and Mary T. Huber, *The Knowledge Industry in the United States* (Princeton, NJ: Princeton University Press, 1986).

b. Marc Porat, *The Information Economy: Definition and Measurement*, OT Special Publication 77-12(1) (U.S. Department of Commerce, 1977), 104–134.

c. John R. Baldwin and Desmond Beckstead, "Knowledge Workers in Canada's Economy, 1971–2001," Statistics Canada Analytical Paper, catalogue number 11-624-MIE—No. 004, October 2003.

d. The U.K. data are reported in Phillip Brown and Anthony Hesketh, *The Mismanagement of Talent* (Oxford: Oxford University Press, 2004).

Within organizations, knowledge workers tend to be closely aligned with the organization's growth prospects. Knowledge workers in management roles come up with new strategies. Knowledge workers in R&D and engineering create new products. Knowledge workers in marketing package products and services in ways that appeal to customers. Without knowledge workers there would be no new products and services, and no growth.

Knowledge Workers and the World Economy

P ETER DRUCKER, who was the first person to describe knowledge workers to any substantial degree (in his 1959 book *Landmarks of Tomorrow*), said as far back as 1969 that:

> To make knowledge work productive will be the great management task of this century, just as to make manual work productive was the great management task of the last century.[a]

Then in 1997 Drucker went even further out along the knowledge worker limb:

> The productivity of knowledge and knowledge workers will not be the only competitive factor in the world economy. It is, however, likely to become the decisive factor, at least for most industries in the developed countries.[b]

Why did Drucker—and why should we—believe that knowledge workers and their productivity were so important to the world economy? There are a variety of reasons. First, they are a large and growing category of workers. If we can't figure out how to make more than a quarter of the labor force more productive, we're going to have prob-

Yet despite the importance of knowledge workers to the economic success of countries, companies, and other groups, they haven't received sufficient attention. We know little about how to improve knowledge workers' performance, which is very unfortunate, because no less an authority than Peter Drucker has said that improving knowledge worker performance is the most important economic issue of the age (see "Knowledge Workers and the World Economy"). So I've chosen to write this book about how we can make knowledge workers more productive and effective at their jobs.

lems with our economy overall. Second, they are the most expensive type of worker that organizations employ, so it's doubly shameful if they're not as productive as they could be.

Third, they are key to the growth of many economies. Agricultural and manufacturing work have generally become commoditized, and are moving to the economies where they can be performed at the lowest cost. The only forms of agricultural or industrial work that survive in sophisticated economies are those in which a high degree of knowledge has been injected—for example, in biotechnology manufacturing, or in "precision farming," in which the fertilizer and pesticides administered to a given crop are carefully monitored using GPS devices in tractors. If agriculture and manufacturing are moving to countries with low labor costs (China is a particularly good example), the jobs that remain in the so-called knowledge-based economies are particularly critical to these countries' economic survival. It's not clear exactly what workers in the United States, Western Europe, and Japan are going to do for a living in the future (other than provide local services), but it is clear that if these economies are to prosper, the jobs of many of the workers must be particularly knowledge-intensive.

a. Peter Drucker, *The Age of Discontinuity* (New York: Harper & Row, 1969).
b. Peter Drucker, "The Future That Has Already Happened," *Harvard Business Review* (September-October 1997): 21.

I have arrived at the topic from two different directions. For about fifteen years I've been doing research on business processes and how they can be improved.[4] I've come to the conclusion that the most important processes for organizations today involve knowledge work. In the past, these haven't really been the focus of most organizations—improving administrative and operational processes has been easier—but they must be in the future. The other starting point has been knowledge management.[5] I've worked with or studied many organizations that have built systems to capture and store knowledge, but the real key to effective use of knowledge is to embed it into the work of knowledge workers. That, of course, leads to a broader interest in how knowledge work can lead to better performance and results.

Over several years I've gathered information from what little is written on the topic, and created or participated in six studies of companies or groups of knowledge workers. Some of the studies were focused on how to use technology to better the lot of the knowledge worker; others were focused on improving knowledge work processes or understanding the effect of the physical workplace on knowledge work. Across these studies I've analyzed or surveyed over a hundred companies and more than six hundred individual knowledge workers. I've also gathered together a large number of case studies and examples of organizations that are addressing this issue.

In this book I'll treat the issue of improving knowledge worker performance from a wide variety of perspectives—organizational and managerial, process, information technology, and even the physical workplace. I believe it's by far the broadest, most comprehensive collection of knowledge on the topic of knowledge work and its improvement. That's not to say that there aren't many other books that need to be written on it—and read—over the coming years. To use a well-worn but apt phrase, I'm just scratching the surface.

What Is a Knowledge Worker?

What is a knowledge worker? I've defined them for well over a decade in the following way:

> Knowledge workers have high degrees of expertise, education, or experience, and the primary purpose of their jobs involves the creation, distribution, or application of knowledge.

Knowledge workers think for a living. They live by their wits—any heavy lifting on the job is intellectual, not physical. They solve problems, they understand and meet the needs of customers, they make decisions, and they collaborate and communicate with other people in the course of doing their own work.

It's easy to point to examples of knowledge workers: physicians and physicists, scientists and sci-fi writers, airplane pilots and airplane designers. We know them when we see them. They don't necessarily have to work in knowledge-intensive industries—managers of any company are knowledge workers, applying knowledge to make decisions in the best interests of their enterprises. Even the most industrial company has engineers, researchers, marketers, and planners. Knowledge workers work in small start-ups and large global corporations. Outside of work, they reside in tony, cool areas of cities and in middle-class or wealthy suburbs; some have moved to resort locations and do their work virtually. For many of you reading this book, virtually everyone you deal with in your job and your social life could be another knowledge worker.

What's difficult is pointing to people who clearly and definitively are not knowledge workers. Most jobs require some degree of knowledge to perform them successfully, and it's probably also true that the number of jobs requiring no knowledge whatsoever has decreased over time. Even if I drive a taxi, I need some geographical knowledge to get by (London taxi drivers, in particular, have to possess "The Knowledge" of its streets before getting their licenses). Even if I take tickets at a movie theater, I need both customer service knowledge and the ability to recognize when someone's trying to sneak in. Even ditch diggers need some knowledge of soil conditions and how to lift shovels full of dirt without hurting their backs. I'm sympathetic to the idea that increasing numbers of workers need knowledge to do their jobs. However, that doesn't necessarily make them knowledge workers.

Definitions of knowledge workers that incorporate anyone who uses knowledge on the job are also not very helpful. Peter Drucker, for example, has defined a knowledge worker as "someone who knows more about his or her job than anyone else in the organization." Drucker was certainly prescient about the fact that knowledge work is becoming more important, and he's right that knowledge workers often understand their own jobs better than others. But this definition also means that taxi drivers, movie ticket takers, and ditch diggers could qualify as knowledge workers to Drucker; his definition also implies that there is only one knowledge worker per job per organization. By my definition, these types of workers don't fully qualify as knowledge workers because creating, distributing, or applying knowledge isn't the primary purpose of their jobs. They only think for a small part of their living.

Whether someone is a knowledge worker or not is admittedly sometimes a matter of degree and interpretation. Many people use knowledge in their jobs and have some degree of education or expertise, but for knowledge workers the role of knowledge must be central to the job, and they must be highly educated or expert. Working with data or information alone isn't enough—it would be difficult to be a knowledge worker, for example, without having a college degree (college dropouts Bill Gates and Michael Dell notwithstanding).

Despite a few necessary shadings in the definition of knowledge workers, it's clear that organizational success depends on the innovativeness and productivity of these workers within their organizations. However, along with adding value, knowledge workers also pose challenges to conventional management wisdom and organizing principles: they are mobile and concerned that their experiences position them well for future opportunities; they are dispersed across the organizational structure and the globe, yet the interdependence and complexity of their work requires them to collaborate effectively with others in different functions, physical locations, time zones, and even organizations; they must command a body of knowledge that needs to be constantly updated; and their work is inherently emergent—the important problems they solve and opportunities they capitalize on are novel and rarely, if ever, standard to the point that the work can become routine. In short, knowledge workers are critical to the success of almost any organization, but they present unique challenges as well.

Knowledge Workers as a Class

Just how unique are the challenges knowledge workers present? Some might argue—and at least one person has—that knowledge workers and knowledge work should be managed in the same way that other work is. This person recently wrote:

> . . . the old dichotomy between manual workers and knowledge workers is not very meaningful . . . fewer and fewer workers perform routine tasks that do not draw upon accumulated knowledge and expertise. To paraphrase Richard Nixon, "We are all knowledge workers now."

He argues instead that knowledge workers should be treated like any other workers in business processes, and that process improvement approaches apply just as well to knowledge workers as to anyone else.

I won't mention that person's name or cite the source of the quote, because I want to use him as an example to prove that he's wrong. He's a management guru, and a knowledge worker *par excellence*. I happen to have worked with him closely for several years. While he argues that knowledge workers' work processes can be addressed just like anyone else's, I have a lot of experience with this fellow's work habits, and they certainly couldn't be improved by handing him a process map and telling him to follow it. Like many knowledge workers, this gent worked with a very high degree of independence and autonomy—even when he ostensibly had an employer. He resisted schedules and often missed deadlines. He was picky, quirky, and cantankerous much of the time. Virtually every time I met with him, the first fifteen minutes of discussion had to be about gossip or politics or books—anything but the task at hand.

Yet when he finally produced, the quality of his work was usually very high—sometimes brilliant. Certainly his work participation and outputs were sufficiently important that I couldn't risk alienating him by criticizing his work habits, or suggesting that they could be made more productive. On most matters (the proper treatment of knowledge workers being an exception) I had considerable respect for his intellect, and dealing with him was generally worth the trouble. However, it's quite ironic for him to argue that knowledge workers are no different from manual, administrative, or production workers, because he embodies everything about knowledge workers that make them different and difficult to manage.

If this example isn't sufficient, throughout the rest of this first chapter and occasionally through the book, I'll describe how knowledge workers are different from other workers. I'll argue that they don't like to be told what to do, that the flow of their work is difficult to structure and predict, that they work best when working with other people in social networks, and that they are better led by example than by explicit management.

It's certainly true that some other types of workers—say, production workers in a manufacturing plant, or a checker in a grocery store chain—share some of these attributes to some degree. Virtually no one, for example, likes to be told what to do. Every day, however, production and retail workers are told precisely what to do ("Tighten those bolts with twenty foot-pounds of torque, not ten"; "You can take your break as soon as you change the register tape"), and their managers and companies generally get away with it. If managers gave similar explicit instructions to their knowledge workers ("Sharpen your pencil before you start that financial plan"), however, it's unlikely that their employees would stay with the company for long. If by some chance they tolerated being managed this way, it's unlikely that they'd give the job their full commitment and intellectual horsepower. This substantial difference in autonomy is only one of the key attributes of knowledge workers, but by itself it's enough to justify treating them as a separate class of workers deserving the separate approaches to performance improvement and management that I'm putting forth in this book.

Common Attributes of Knowledge Work and Knowledge Workers

The fact that knowledge workers primarily rely on their brains rather than on their bodies in their jobs means that they have some attributes in common. These aren't terribly surprising, and they all follow from a few basic principles and observations, but they need to be stated. Most derive from the fact that knowledge work is less structured, and perhaps less structurable, than administrative or production work. As John Seely Brown and Paul Duguid have described this distinction:

> In such areas, life is less linear; inputs and outputs are less well defined; and information is less "targeted." These are, rather, areas where making sense, interpreting, and understanding are both problematic and highly valued—areas where, above all, meaning and knowledge are at a premium.[6]

This is an excellent characterization of knowledge work in comparison to its predecessor forms of toil.

The basic principles and observations follow.

Knowledge workers like autonomy. One important aspect of knowledge workers is that they don't like to be told what to do. Thinking for a living engenders thinking for oneself. Knowledge workers are paid for their education, experience, and expertise, so it is not surprising that they often take offense when someone else rides roughshod over their intellectual territory. Of course, knowledge workers don't like their work to be ignored, and there are some things they like to be told, such as the broader significance and implications of their tasks and jobs.

This autonomy is in part a natural result of the nature of knowledge work. Since it's difficult to tell whether knowledge workers are actually thinking at any given moment, supervisors pretty much have to take their word for it. The outputs of knowledge work are also difficult to specify in great detail, so that is generally left up to the workers.

Autonomy is also viewed by knowledge workers as a fair exchange for the amount of education and training they have received. Some research has suggested that scientists and engineers view autonomy on the job as the major reason why they worked hard in college and graduate school. And with increased education presumably comes a greater ability to manage oneself.

There are several different domains in which knowledge workers prefer autonomy. In particular, they would like autonomy as to the detailed processes they follow in doing their work. Tell them what they need to get done and when it needs to be finished, and they will, if they have their preference, figure out the details. They know the circumstances in which they think best. They also like to decide their own work locations and schedules. If a computer programmer tells the boss that he is most productive working from 8 p.m. to 4 a.m., a smart boss would try to facilitate that arrangement.

For the most part, knowledge workers have gotten the autonomy they want. Since they own their means of production—their brains and knowledge—it would be difficult for organizations to deny them that autonomy. Professional associations of knowledge workers have also sometimes resisted attempts to apply too much control in the workplace. For example, the American Medical Association has often struggled in the courts with hospitals over physician and medical staff autonomy. There has also generally been a good labor market for knowledge workers, so they have been able to change jobs to find more autonomy if necessary.

However, because knowledge workers prefer autonomy doesn't mean they should always be given the maximum amount of it. As I will mention throughout this book, some efforts to improve knowledge worker performance may involve removing some discretion from the knowledge worker. Still, organizations must be careful when implementing any new process or technology that significantly reduces the autonomy of their knowledge workers.

Specifying the detailed steps and flow of knowledge-intensive processes is less valuable and more difficult than for other types of work. This is a corollary of my first generalization about knowledge work. Knowledge workers don't like to be told what to do, and they also don't like to see their jobs reduced to a series of boxes and arrows.

Typically, when we want to improve performance we begin by breaking down the structure of the task into its constituent elements. This has been the case at least since Frederick Taylor's day, if not before. The idea is that when broken into piece-parts, knowledge work processes can be more easily followed and measured, and unnecessary steps eliminated altogether. However, this approach often doesn't work very well for knowledge work and workers. In my experience, knowledge workers will often resist describing the steps they follow to carry out an assignment. The more complex and knowledge-intensive the work, the more likely this will be true. Perhaps there are so many variations that describing the typical flow of work is impossible. Knowledge work also often involves a high degree of iterative collaboration among knowledge workers, and this may be difficult to describe or model.

Even if you can get a knowledge worker to describe his or her work process, it may not be a very helpful description. First, the work flow may not be very similar to another worker's description of the supposedly same process. Second, the steps may seem maddeningly inefficient: "First I come up with an idea. Then I think about it for a while. Then I talk to my lab partner about it. Then I think about the reactions she's given me." Such a process would be anathema to a stopwatch-packing Taylorist, but it's often how knowledge workers—particularly those involved in knowledge creation activities—work.

So does this mean that we have to give up on taking a process perspective on improving knowledge work? No. Despite the lack of value from analyzing process workflows in detail, there are still plenty of other process tools available to potential improvers of knowledge work. I will describe these in chapter 4. One, however, is the next generalization I'll make about this type of work.

"You can observe a lot by watching." Lawrence Peter Berra had it right—a natural follow-on to the previous attribute of knowledge workers is that if you can't get them to describe their work in detail, you have to observe it in detail. Systematic observation—also known as "shadowing" or "ethnography"—is often an effective way to understand how knowledge workers do their work.

Observation can be undertaken through a variety of means. The most common is to have an observer "shadow" or follow around one or more knowledge workers. It's also possible to have the observer participate in the work process—called "participant observation." The observer can obviously learn a great deal about the work by doing it, and participation can also increase trust levels. Finally, some observation takes place through videotaping and later analysis of the work process, though this approach is hardly conducive to trust.

There are several reasons why observation is well suited to understanding knowledge work. One, since thinking is invisible, "hanging out" with knowledge workers as they do their work will give the observer a better sense of what is really going on. The observer can hear the casual comments, the jokes, and the complaints of knowledge workers firsthand, and use them to piece together a story of the work. Two, spending time with knowledge workers increases their trust in the observer, and may lead to more disclosure about the nature of their work.

But this approach to understanding knowledge work has significant drawbacks. Paying for a human observer is expensive, and it may require substantial time for an observer to gain the trust of knowledge workers and fully understand their work. Nevertheless, without observation, it's unlikely that the work can be penetrated.

Of course, there are also ethical considerations to observation. A group of knowledge workers shouldn't be observed unless all the objectives and intentions of the observation are fully disclosed. I've found that knowledge workers are usually quite willing to welcome and discuss their work with an observer if they feel the observation is intended to help them, but nothing makes them clam up faster than a suspicion that the observation will have negative consequences.

Knowledge workers usually have good reasons for doing what they do. In the days of business process reengineering, we assumed that smart analysts could quickly figure out better ways of doing work. This was, in fact, often true. Nobody had ever thought about many administrative and operational processes before, and improvements were easily identified.

It's not so easy with knowledge work, which is one of the reasons why we have to observe it closely. Knowledge workers have typically thought about why and how they do their work, and may have themselves made many of the obvious improvements to it. There is probably a reason behind almost everything they undertake (or at minimum a logical rationalization). If improvements are going to be identified, it's probably only after serious and deep study. Julian Orr, an anthropologist who has studied technical service representatives, argues that analysts of such work are rarely sufficiently "concerned with work practice . . . they do not focus on what is done in accomplishing a given job."[7]

So for knowledge work, we need to take workers at their word—or more importantly, their deed. We must be careful before assuming that chatting with other workers is wasted time, or that time spent cogitating can be eliminated without consequences. It's usually safer to assume that work is done a certain way for good reason than to assume it can be quickly and easily changed.

Commitment matters. In the industrial economy, one could do a job with one's body even when the brain and heart weren't committed to the job. But this isn't the case for knowledge work. It's unlikely that you'll get great performance out of a knowledge worker if he or she isn't mentally and emotionally committed to the job.

This fact has a number of ramifications. Chief among them is that knowledge workers need some say in what they work on and how they do it. There is nothing that limits commitment like being told what to work on by someone else. This factor is behind, for example, the famous 3M approach of giving researchers 15 percent of their time to work independently on something they think is important to the company. Obviously knowledge workers are generally willing to do some things that others ask (or even tell) them to do, but a degree of voluntarism helps a lot.

Another factor affecting commitment is a perception of "fair process." As the strategy academics Chan Kim and Renée Mauborgne have pointed out, workers—and particularly knowledge workers—care not only about the fairness of outcomes, but also about the fairness of the process used to arrive at outcomes:

> Fair process turns out to be a powerful management tool for companies struggling to make the transition from a production-based to a knowledge-based economy, in which value creation depends increasingly on ideas and innovation. Fair process profoundly influences attitudes and behaviors critical to high performance. It builds trust and unlocks ideas.[8]

If high levels of commitment are going to be maintained, managers of people who think for a living need to acknowledge the fact that workers can sometimes think better than their bosses. The manager or executive may have a better grasp of the strategy or the big picture of the business, but the knowledge worker may know the details of his or her field much better. Having a manager pretend to know everything can be very damaging to an expert's commitment and loyalty.

Knowledge workers value their knowledge, and don't share it easily. Knowledge is all that knowledge workers have—it's the tool of their trade, the means of their production. It's therefore natural that they would have difficulty relinquishing or sharing it in such a way that their own jobs might be threatened.

In the early days of knowledge management, when companies were beginning to talk about sharing knowledge within and across organizations, I used to say, "Sharing knowledge is an unnatural act." I also mentioned that, "Of course, unnatural acts are committed every day." Companies just needed to put the necessary incentives and assurances in place to ensure that people were willing to share their knowledge.

If anything, a knowledge worker's concerns about sharing have become even more justified in the last few years. In addition to the usual fears of layoffs, some clueless companies have been asking their workers to train their offshore successors before they lose their jobs. Almost every knowledge worker is wondering whether his or her job could be the next to move to India or China. It's enough to give anyone pause about contributing knowledge to some other worker or a knowledge repository. Again, this doesn't mean that we can't design organizations and processes in such a way that knowledge will flow across organizations. We just have to acknowledge that knowledge workers will view their knowledge as a highly valuable asset, and that they will be reluctant to share it without rewards and/or guarantees of continued employment.

There are other precedents for this problem in organizations. For years companies have tried to make the customer information of their salespeople an organizational, rather than an individual, asset. Sales forces have worked just as diligently to withhold what they know about their customers, often resisting adding it to the "customer relationship management" systems their organizations have implemented. Many organizations have added policies and procedures that reassure the sales force that they'll still own the customer information and knowledge while they work for the company. Smart organizations will put similar approaches in place for the knowledge assets of their knowledge workers.

Implications of These Attributes

The implication of these attributes is that knowledge workers can't be "managed" in the traditional sense of the word. As Warren Bennis has pointed out, they bear a peculiar resemblance to cats, which as we know can't be herded.[9] Some of the attributes of knowledge workers sound like T. S. Eliot's descriptions of the contrary cat, the Rum Tum Tugger:

For he will do
As he do do,
And there's no doing anything about it! . . .
When you let him in, then he wants out,
He's always in the wrong side of the door, . . .
For he only likes what he finds for himself, . . .
The Rum Tum Tugger is artful and knowing . . .[10]

Bennis argues that this type of individual can only be led, not managed, by visionary, inspirational leaders who build trust and mutual respect in their organizations. This is no doubt the case, and I discuss some aspects of this leadership in chapter 9 (no doubt with less expertise and grace than Bennis would).

But visionary leaders are often in short supply, and I believe there are other ways in which we can intervene in—and improve—knowledge work. As with any other type of work, there are many potential avenues to betterment. In addition to better leadership and management, in this book I describe at least five other approaches to helping people who think for a living.

What's Coming in This Book

Thus far I've described what knowledge workers are, why they're important, and some of the things they have in common. In the next chapter I'll describe how they differ. Both the similarities and differences form an important set of baseline factors to consider when attempting to improve knowledge work. That subject—improvement—forms the basis for the other chapters. In chapter 3, I'll describe the subject of improvement or interventions in general—the case for intervening in the first place, how to measure improvement, and common mistakes that organizations make in their interventions. In each subsequent chapter I'll describe a particular approach to intervening in and improving knowledge work. Chapter 4 talks about the roles of process and measurement. Chapter 5 describes technology provided by organizations as a means of improving knowledge work, while chapter 6 focuses on technology, information, and knowledge management at the personal level. Chapter 7 describes the social networks of high-performing knowledge workers. Chapter 8 describes the physical workspace for knowledge work. Chapter 9 focuses on how to be an effective manager of knowledge work and workers.

At the end of each chapter I will point out the implications of the subject treated for managers wishing to extract better performance and results from knowledge workers. These sections provide a quick summary of the recommendations in the chapter, but of course they don't provide the context, the examples, and deeper analysis.

Recommendations for Getting Results from Knowledge Workers

- All jobs involve knowledge to some degree, but knowledge workers are those whose jobs are particularly knowledge-oriented. The recommendations in this book apply to those expert workers in jobs whose primary purpose is to create, distribute, or apply knowledge.

- Knowledge workers differ from other kinds of workers in their autonomy, motivations, and attitudes.

- Knowledge workers enjoy their autonomy, so be careful about improvement approaches that impinge upon it—although sometimes this may be necessary.

- Knowledge work tends to be unstructured. Specifying a detailed flow of work is sometimes possible, but is probably not the best way to improve a knowledge work process.

- Knowledge work often needs to be observed in some detail and at some length before it can be truly understood.

- Knowledge workers are usually intelligent, so be careful about assuming that a particular work task is unnecessary, or that a work process can be improved upon easily.

- Commitment matters to knowledge work. Don't do anything to damage the knowledge worker's commitment to the job and to the organization.

How Knowledge Workers Differ, and the Difference It Makes

As I stated in chapter 1, despite having a number of traits in common, all knowledge workers aren't alike. A computer programmer and a physician, for example, are both knowledge workers, but they have very different educational backgrounds, working conditions, business processes, and measures of effectiveness and success. Therefore, an approach to classifying knowledge workers may help organizations determine how best to manage, measure, and improve their work. This classification serves a useful purpose if it passes two tests. First, it should be easy to apply; putting any given type of worker into one of the classes should not require great amounts of work or mental gyrations. Second, the classification should be useful in improving the performance of knowledge workers when some intervention is attempted. Otherwise, the distinction makes no difference.

Distinguishing Among Kinds of Knowledge Workers in Your Organization

One important purpose for distinguishing among knowledge workers is that organizations can't improve all knowledge worker roles at once. They have to make choices about which knowledge-oriented jobs to address at any given time. Understanding the distinctions among knowledge workers begins to provide a basis for choosing among them when some prioritization is necessary. I have tried for years to develop the "perfect matrix" for distinguishing among knowledge workers, and have come to the conclusion that it doesn't exist. There are simply too many important ways in which knowledge work differs to reduce the variations to two dimensions. However, I do think that some dimensions are more important than others, and the matrix I'll describe next has been very handy in terms of shaping an intervention for different types of knowledge work.

Distinguishing on Judgment and Collaboration

The matrix in figure 2-1 is an example of a classification approach; it uses the level of work complexity (the interpretation and judgment required in the process) and the degree of collaboration required as classification dimensions.[1] These dimensions are important because the level of collaboration often drives the degree of structure and computer mediation that's possible in a particular job, and the level of complexity of the work can dictate how much knowledge is required to perform it successfully.

A *transaction* worker, for example, might be found in a call center. An *integration* process example might be an information system development operation. An investment bank might provide an example for the *collaboration* model, and a primary-care physician would practice with the *expert* model. I have found these distinctions useful in determining what kind of interventions make sense for the different cells of the matrix.

FIGURE 2-1

A classification structure for knowledge-intensive processes

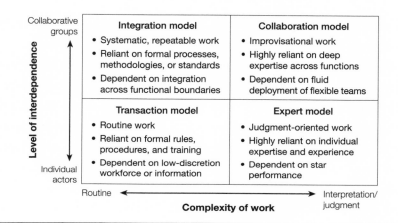

It might be very reasonable, for example, to create a script for transaction workers to read to their customers or to use in preparing or assembling a product or service. Work requiring more judgment and collaboration, however, wouldn't benefit from such a script. It would probably be impossible, for example, to prepare a script that would anticipate all of the contingencies and activities that could take place in a major corporate legal transaction such as a merger or acquisition.

Because integration work is relatively structured, it is often possible to reuse knowledge assets (in fact, "scripting" is the most structured form of reuse), and this work is often the subject of efforts to capture such knowledge for reuse. For example, companies doing software development try to get programmers to store their code in libraries for use in other programming. Automobile companies try to get lower-level designers and engineers to reuse certain component designs, rather than inventing new ones. Reuse would probably be less successful in more expert and collaborative work.

Because expert work is largely done by individuals, it is sometimes possible to use a computer to mediate the work process and inject organizational knowledge into it. I will describe a successful example of this type of intervention in the health care industry in chapter 4. Still, because experts *are* experts who value their own knowledge particularly highly, it can be particularly difficult to get them to use someone else's knowledge.

Collaboration work is perhaps the most difficult to improve in any structured way, because this type of work feels very iterative and improvisational to those who do it. For example, if you ask an investment banker to describe his or her work process (and I've done this a few times), you'll typically be told that there is no process—the work is different every day. This work is often done by highly educated (and compensated) professionals, so it's particularly difficult to get them to do things in a new way that someone else has prescribed. Typically, the types of interventions that organizations make into this type of work involve the manipulation of external factors, which might include putting workers together in teams, co-locating them, or making more knowledge available to them—in a knowledge management repository, for example.

I'll refer back to this matrix a number of times when I begin to describe particular approaches to improving knowledge work. However, it's clear that no one or two dimensions can capture all the complexity of knowledge-intensive processes. The following are some other dimensions that may be useful in classifying them.

Distinguishing on Knowledge Activity

Knowledge workers can either find knowledge, create it, package it, distribute it, or apply it. The particular role that a worker plays relative to knowledge often has implications for how the activity can be changed or improved. A job in which knowledge is created should be treated very differently from one in which it is applied.

Those who *find* existing knowledge need to understand knowledge requirements, search for it among multiple sources, and pass it along to the requester or user. Examples might include a librarian or a competitive intelligence analyst. Many organizations now expect all knowledge workers to find knowledge themselves, but in order for this to work well there must be a considerable amount of training—which there usually isn't. The relationship between the finder and user of knowledge is a key factor in the success of knowledge-finding processes.

Other workers *create* new knowledge. Examples include the researchers in a pharmaceutical firm, creative directors in advertising, or authors of books and movie screenplays. Knowledge creation is perhaps the most difficult knowledge activity to structure and improve, since much of it takes place in the brains of knowledge workers. Yet leaving these workers alone isn't the answer either; their productivity and performance is critical to the success of organizations in the knowledge economy. The productivity and effectiveness of knowledge creators can often be improved by giving them easy access to previously created knowledge that can be reused, or to analyses of what happened in earlier situations when similar knowledge was created.

Knowledge *packagers* put together knowledge created by others. Publishing is a prime example of knowledge packaging. Packaging is often designed to make the work of other knowledge workers more efficient—we read a newspaper packaged by reporters and editors, for example, so that we don't have to read all the wire services. Even though they do not generally create *new* knowledge, the editing, design, and proofing processes qualify as knowledge work. One of the things that often makes packaging less efficient than it could be is that the packagers must often wait for the knowledge to be created, or can't rely on the creators to finish on time (it wasn't a great surprise to my publisher, for example, to learn that this book would be late!).

Those who work professionally with knowledge management are most frequently *distributors* of knowledge. They create systems and processes to increase access to knowledge for others, and get it to those who need it. There may not be enough distributors in an organization to worry about redesigning their jobs, but these roles may be critical enablers of interventions involving other types of knowledge workers.

At the end of the knowledge line are those who *apply* knowledge. These knowledge workers use and reuse knowledge in the course of their work, but don't generally create a lot of new knowledge (though every good worker creates some). Examples include accountants and auditors, most low-level professionals, and lower-level health care practitioners. These workers are often quite numerous within organizations, and are thus frequently the target of change programs.

Distinguishing by Type of Idea

Knowledge workers can also be distinguished by the types of ideas with which they deal. While the scope and scale of ideas undoubtedly represent a continuum, let's split them into big ideas and small ones. Big ideas are those that dramatically change people and organizations—ideas for new products, services, business models, and strategic directions. "We should develop a computer with a point-and-click operating system that's much easier to use than any other," is an example of big idea knowledge; it was someone's thinking, perhaps Steve Jobs's, at Apple Computer in the mid-1980s. By definition, an organization can pursue relatively few of these big ideas because they require a lot of time and effort to implement.

Then there are the small ideas. These are minor improvements in what organizations produce or how they work. "Let's put glass shelves in our refrigerators so that customers can see through them into the back," is an example of the type of small ideas that are generated every day—either in products or processes. In the world of process ideas, small ideas are analogous to quality management and continuous process improvement; big ideas are analogous to process innovation—the start-from-scratch, think-out-of-the-box approach to change.

To which types of knowledge and knowledge work should organizations aspire? The most conventional view would be that only a small proportion of workers should be creators of big ideas. Workers have traditionally been viewed as users, not creators, of ideas, and if they do create ideas they have generally been small ones. It's only researchers and senior managers to whom organizations have turned for big idea creation.

My view, however, is that the organizations that will be most successful in the future will be those in which it's everyone's job to be creating and using both big and small ideas. Certainly frontline workers should continue to practice continuous improvement and refinement of their own job activities, but why shouldn't they also continuously propose new products, processes, business models, strategies, etc.? They may not want to call the CEO every time they have a big idea, but there should be processes for prioritizing and filtering large and small ideas. Surely the most innovative and profitable firms will be those in which everyone thinks at all levels.

There are a few examples of firms in which it's everybody's job—at least almost everybody's—to think. Some are knowledge-intensive firms, like consulting or pharmaceutical development, in which professionals or researchers are all expected to create knowledge. It's much less common to find such an orientation in industrial firms, which is why Chaparral Steel is so unusual.[2] In this Texas-based firm, thinking is clearly everyone's job. Even the first-line associate is expected to work on production experiments, to identify new product offerings, and to propose new process designs, although it's unusual to find steel-workers who want to be knowledge workers. Because of this policy, Chaparral is highly productive relative to other steel companies. Most important from my perspective, Chaparral has a very different style of management (from most steel companies) in which all workers are treated as knowledge workers—the culture is nonhierarchical and workers are trusted to produce at high levels without monitoring.

Differentiating on Cost and Scale

The cost of performing knowledge work may make a difference to how much effort is put into managing or improving it. The cost is driven both by the compensation paid to workers in a particular role and the number of these workers within an organization. The most expensive knowledge workers are typically those with the most education and seniority—hence the most difficult to change in many cases.

The larger the number of people in a particular knowledge work job, the greater the degree of difficulty in managing, improving, or changing it. Greater scale means that more people have to be retrained and change their behavior. However, processes involving a high number of people may be more worthy of investment in improvement initiatives. British Telecom (BT), for example, decided that one of its most important knowledge jobs was the customer service representative in the call center—a job BT refers to as "adviser." BT has fifteen thousand such advisers. Although the job is an important one in terms of customer satisfaction, the simple numbers of employees in the role made a compelling case for investment. I'll describe the intervention BT made for its advisers in chapter 4.

Differentiating on Process Attributes

Knowledge workers also differ by the nature of the work process they perform.[3] I won't go into detail on process interventions here, because that's the subject of chapter 3. But process characteristics could dictate which process segments to address in which order. For example, the work in a knowledge-intensive process could be parallel, with all workers performing the entire process and all steps taking place at the same time (e.g., call centers). This makes the process relatively easy to monitor. Some knowledge work processes are sequential, and workers may perform only one or two steps in the process (e.g., commercial credit approval). One common improvement approach for sequential processes is to entrust the entire sequence to a single worker—often known as a "case manager"—supported by a dedicated information system. This improvement approach has been frequently employed in life insurance underwriting processes.[4]

Knowledge work also varies by the degree of recurrence of specific tasks. The work may be a project with a low recurrence rate (e.g., industrial design for a product). Alternatively, it may be fairly repetitious (e.g., credit card fraud detection). Repetition, of course, makes it easier to determine and redesign the structure of work. In many cases it may even be possible to automate much of the process if it's highly repetitive.

Another process attribute distinguishing knowledge work and workers is the degree of inputs required for the successful performance of the process. Some knowledge work may need very high volumes of daily data input (e.g., claims processing), while others don't need much (e.g., market research, editing of documents).

Finally, some knowledge work processes are easier to measure than others. For some processes, metrics are easy to develop (e.g., medical coding). Others are difficult to measure in any way other than a qualitative sense (e.g., patent search and filings, market research). The variable ability to measure can make a difference to management, improvement, and outsourcing (e.g., the development of service-level agreements) initiatives.

Differentiating on Business Criticality

As with manufacturing and operational jobs, some knowledge workers are simply more critical to the business than others. Which jobs, for example, are most important to bringing in new revenue to a business? How strong a fit is there between a particular job and the strategy of the organization? How much does the daily performance of the business depend on how well the process is performed?

The same knowledge work job may be much more important to one organization than another. A programmer in a bank, for example, may matter much less to the success of the organization than a programmer doing similar work for a software company. A financial analyst may be relatively tangential in a manufacturing company, but mission-critical in a mutual funds company.

The importance of a job is not the same as its status or how much the workers in it are paid. A telephone repairperson, for example, isn't paid much or accorded much status, but can be very important to a company's reputation for customer service.

Differentiating on Mobility

Some knowledge workers stay in one place, and others move around a lot. Fine, but what difference does it make? Many companies have found that whether a worker is mobile is a critical factor in job design. Mobility can influence what kind of office a knowledge worker needs, the types of technology he or she will employ, the relative ability to observe the worker's performance, and the ease of communicating with the worker. Sometimes mobility can be a critical element in design of a particular knowledge work process. For example, should the process be performed in one place (e.g., mortgage approvals at a bank headquarters) or in mobile locations (e.g., mortgage approvals at the client site)?

Over the last decade or so, with advances in mobile information technology, the trend has been to allow or structure more and more mobility into knowledge workers' jobs. I recently heard about a consulting firm that promised to pay its workers several hundred dollars in extra compensation if they promised not to visit the office more than three days a week! Such moves have been undertaken for two primary reasons: cost reduction and greater flexibility for employees. I have seen them succeed on both counts.

However, as I'll discuss in chapter 7, there is a cost to knowledge worker mobility. As my friends and coauthors Don Cohen and Larry Prusak point out in their book *In Good Company*, mobile work doesn't build social capital or social networks.[5] If you care about how well your knowledge workers share their knowledge, be careful about dramatically increasing their level of mobility.

Segmenting on Knowledge
Worker Differences

Because it's impossible to intervene in all forms of knowledge work within an organization at once and to treat all knowledge workers alike when attempting to improve work, it's a good idea for organizations to have a segmentation strategy for knowledge workers. Such a strategy would describe the different types of knowledge workers in the organization and how they differ. It would also address which knowledge work jobs are most critical to the achievement of the organization's strategy, and prioritize them for analysis and intervention.

The segmentation may be based on any of the criteria described above. After meaningful segments have been developed, it makes sense to apply IT, process improvement approaches, and other productivity aids differently for each category.

The question is what sort of segmentation scheme to use. A new "eWorkforce" group at Intel, for example, has created one based primarily on mobility and behaviors and attitudes toward technology. Its categories are as follows:

- *Functionalists:* Primarily manufacturing (there are some office workers here, however) workers who use information technology occasionally, but do no rely heavily on "office IT" to perform their job functions

- *Cube captains:* Spend the majority of their time in the office, are very mainstream in their office IT needs, and are overall very happy with the tool sets they have

- *Nomads:* Heavy users of remote access; whether while traveling or working in remote offices, they need mobility in their IT environments

- *Global collaborators:* Interface often with people around the world; they have elements of the nomad segment, but they work across time zones and do a lot of collaboration and hence need access to collaboration tools anywhere, anytime

- *Tech individualists:* They want and need the latest IT tools and are willing to take risks with them; are also often early adopters

These probably wouldn't be the right categories for all organizations, but I view it as a great step forward for Intel to create and address them. Intel is also attempting to put these corporatewide categories into the context of business process and business unit needs.

It's still the early days for segmentation, but my own hypothesis is that the best primary basis for segmenting knowledge workers will be by the job roles they perform within the organization. I would guess that whether you're a field sales analyst or a midlevel marketing manager would drive—more than any other factor—the type of work you do and how it could be done more productively and effectively. Of course, segmentation will be difficult and perhaps expensive. Most organizations don't even know how many different job roles they have. I suspect the only role-based segments that might make sense to single out are those in which there are many workers, or in which better productivity or performance are mission-critical.

One organization that is aggressively pursuing this role-based segmentation of knowledge work is MWH Global, a global engineering, construction, and technology firm. MWH has over six thousand professionals, but executives there have concluded that the best way to make them more productive and knowledgeable is to focus on specific roles. Five mission-critical roles have been identified for an initial intervention, including:

- Business unit leader

- Business developer

- Project manager

- Client service manager

- Technologist

To better understand these roles, MWH is conducting focus groups with each role across each of its geographical regions, doing psychometric testing, analyzing variations in performance within the role, surveying those who perform the role, and correlating key behavioral traits to performance. The results will be used to develop a recruiting profile and a performance management process for each role. MWH also plans to develop a separate "knowledge portal" for each role, with only the knowledge relevant to the role. This comprehensive intervention is made more feasible by the presence of an executive position called "Chief People and Knowledge Officer" to oversee human resource and information technology strategy, learning and development, and knowledge management.

Summary

I have described the nature of knowledge work overall in chapter 1, and some of the key differences across knowledge worker types in this chapter. These chapters will be useful background for the rest of the book. But the application of these ideas—the improvement of knowledge work—is the heart of this book, and you're probably anxious to get to that issue. I'll jump into that in chapter 3 by discussing the topic of interventions in general, and later chapters will address particular types of interventions.

Recommendations for Getting Results from Knowledge Workers

- It's important to recognize the differences among knowledge workers. A matrix of four types based on the degree of collaboration and expertise required in the job is particularly useful in shaping interventions into knowledge work.

- The type of knowledge activity involved in the job (finding, creating, packaging, distributing, and applying) can also dictate different approaches to improving knowledge work.

- It makes sense to apply knowledge work interventions to jobs with the most expensive workers and to those that account for the greatest numbers of employees in an organization.

- Because all knowledge work jobs can't be improved at once, a key element of improvement is to develop a segmentation scheme, with some prioritization of which types of jobs will be addressed in what order.

3

Interventions, Measures, and Experiments in Knowledge Work

It may seem obvious that we're not going to get better performance and results from knowledge workers unless we somehow intervene in their work. But we've avoided doing so in the past. As Peter Drucker notes, we have not generally focused on knowledge worker productivity or performance. He recently commented, "Nobody has really looked at productivity in white collar work in a scientific way. But whenever we do look at it, it is grotesquely unproductive."[1] The dominant approach has been to rely on their individual brains alone, rather than on any approach to improving work. I often say that the typical way of dealing with knowledge workers is to HSPALTA, or "hire smart people and leave them alone."

To Intervene or Not?

We have left knowledge workers alone across many knowledge work professions over decades, and even centuries in some cases. Professors, for example, have their scholarship (and, to a lesser degree, teaching) measured after five to seven years, and then, assuming they are successful, they get tenure and are never seriously assessed again. Researchers in scientific settings such as pharmaceutical firms may work for many years without ever creating a drug that reaches the market. We know that some programmers are ten times more productive than others, but—aside from trying to ensure that the highly productive ones stay in our employ—we don't do anything to analyze the differences between the most productive and the least, and to spread the traits leading to high performance.

I recently visited a semiconductor company that illustrated perfectly this laissez-faire approach. The company has been successful in a variety of markets and has more than twenty different product lines. Each has its own set of dedicated researchers and engineers that designs and develops new products in that line. Yet some product lines are more successful than others—more profitable, with products that are better received by customers, and more likely to incorporate state-of-the-art knowledge and expertise. I asked a group of the company's executives why some product teams did better, and there was a surprising lack of agreement. One said that it was because the most productive groups had their own offices in a separate physical facility. Another felt that they had simply recruited better people. Another suggested that some groups reused their circuit designs more frequently and effectively than others, and hence had higher productivity. One argued strongly that all groups could have been equally productive, but that the CEO had blessed some with more funding and resources than others.

These managers agreed that the high performance of the most successful product-line groups was absolutely critical to their success. Yet they somewhat sheepishly admitted that they had no idea what really caused the variations in group performance. Despite the variations, they hadn't explicitly identified some groups as being higher-performing than others, or ever seriously studied how any of the groups went about their work. But if they could identify what made some groups perform better than others, it's very plausible that they could nurture these factors in the lower-performing groups and improve the entire company's performance. This potential for substantially improved organizational performance is by far the best argument for beginning to penetrate the "black box" of knowledge worker performance.

The executives agreed that in addition to the electrical engineering they performed so frequently, they needed to undertake some "social engineering" to understand better what was going on within and among the different product line groups. What could the company do? There were a variety of possibilities. One would be to simply observe these groups for a period, and ideally contrast the conclusions drawn from the most successful with those derived from the observation of some less successful groups. One could also classify all the ways in which the groups differ, including the leadership and management styles, locational factors, technologies employed, social networks, and so on. A third approach—best undertaken after some initial analysis— would be to pilot an intervention in the lower-performing groups to understand if it brought their performance up.

There are both micro- and macro-level cases for intervening in knowledge work. At the micro level of individual organizations and managers, the case is clear-cut: you need better results, and knowledge workers are the key to those results. You need to get better performance out of them or your business will suffer. Doing nothing will yield no change. Everybody else has already been squeezed, so now it's the knowledge worker's turn.

At the macro level, there may have been good reasons for leaving knowledge workers to their own devices in the past, but they are no longer tenable. Knowledge workers haven't had many interventions in part because their work is difficult to measure, and if there is no measurement, there is no pressure to perform at a faster or even standard rate. However, as I argue later in this chapter, it's possible to come up with measures for any given type of knowledge work, even though there may be no universal measure.

Knowledge workers have also been given a high degree of latitude because their work is for the most part invisible. If you're my boss and you're trying to determine how productive I am, it's hard to tell just by looking at me. Much of my job will involve thinking, and you won't have a clue whether I am thinking seriously about work at any given moment. If I tell you that I do my most productive thinking in the shower, you probably have to take my word for it—and perhaps encourage me to spend more time there. Again, however, there are widely accepted practices involving long-term observation and even participation in knowledge work—forms of ethnography or "corporate anthropology"—that do allow analysts to begin to understand invisible knowledge work.

Finally, knowledge workers are left alone in part because of their power and importance within organizations. They don't particularly welcome being told what to do, and managers don't intervene because they don't want to antagonize these important people. In some cases, professional associations have successfully resisted measures of or interventions into particular types of knowledge work. The workplace practices of doctors and teachers, for example, are protected by their professional associations.

But we can't continue to ignore or take for granted the productivity and effectiveness of knowledge work, for it has become the key to the success of our economy. When we had an agricultural economy, new machines and techniques made that economy much more productive and successful. When ours was a manufacturing-oriented economy, it was critical to assess and improve the productivity and quality of manufacturing processes. Now that our economy is largely based on knowledge work, we need to ensure that we're doing it in the best manner possible, or our economic pursuits cannot thrive.

We can already see the strain from not making knowledge work more productive in our economy. When agricultural and industrial organizations improved productivity, their products became cheaper and more affordable. Most material goods have fallen in price—or at least in the number of work hours needed to procure them—because of these efficiencies. But some knowledge-intensive industries haven't improved productivity very much. Health care organizations haven't reduced the labor necessary to treat a patient. Educational institutions, with only a few exceptions (including the University of Phoenix and a few other online institutions), have not reduced the amount of human activity needed to educate a student. Pharmaceutical firms haven't figured out how to develop drugs more cheaply. As a result, many people find these industries' products and services too expensive, and their cost has increased substantially above the inflation rate. If knowledge-based products and services are to be affordable, we have to figure out how to make knowledge workers more productive.

There is another important analogy to agricultural and industrial work that helps make the case for improving knowledge work productivity and performance; it's the mobility of that work. Agricultural and industrial work has eventually migrated to the countries and regions that do it most cheaply and productively. Agricultural work mobility has been somewhat limited by the fact that food is perishable, but it too has become a global industry. Brazil, for example, produces about 40 percent more orange juice than Florida, and it exports juice around the world. The labor productivity of Brazilian farm workers is substantially better than those in Florida—primarily because of cheaper labor.

In manufacturing, of course, it's an old story that the work flows to the cheapest location around the world. In the Boston area, where I live, textile manufacturing once thrived in mill towns such as Lowell,

Lawrence, Maynard, and Fall River. Then it moved to the southeastern United States. Then it moved to Asia, where it still resides for the moment.

Because knowledge work is invisible and based on trust, it used to be less mobile. It didn't make sense to send your computer programming or product design halfway around the world to be performed by knowledge workers who are paid much less than those in America, Europe, or Japan. Today, however, knowledge work has also become mobile. The Internet and global telecommunications have increased levels of communication with people we cannot see. And growing standards for knowledge work (particularly in computer programming) have lowered the level of trust necessary to contract with someone you don't know. Thus the movement of knowledge work "offshore," which began with call centers and the more structured forms of knowledge work, but now encompasses consulting and systems integration, product design and engineering, and even medical processes, including diagnosis and interpretation of X-rays and CAT scans.

Now that much knowledge work can go anywhere, what will keep it at home? Perhaps the only sure way for a society to retain and grow its knowledge work is to simply be more productive at that work than any global competitor. Other economies may pay their knowledge workers less, but if America or Europe or Japan can offer knowledge work with a higher ratio of quality outputs to inputs, these economies will not lose work to India or China. Therefore, exactly how to improve knowledge work productivity becomes one of the most important economic issues of our time.

With so much at stake, it's clear that the long period during which we took a laissez-faire attitude toward knowledge work must soon come to an end. Of course, manual workers were at one time left alone as well. Their societies made the implicit assumption that they knew what they were doing and were working as hard as they could, just as we do today for knowledge workers. But then came Frederick Taylor in the 1880s and, a couple of decades later, the devotees of "scientific management." Taylor and his adherents, despite a somewhat negative reputation, did some useful things for industrial work, and were generally interested in improving both the lot of manual workers and their relations with management. They figured out how to measure labor productivity, albeit somewhat crudely. They broke manual labor down into its core components. They began to create rules of thumb for how to improve it. While falling short of the label "scientific," their approach to manual labor was the first successful attempt to make it more productive, and to some degree we have relied on their methods for over a hundred years. Peter Drucker even argues that Taylor's work prevented the class wars predicted by Marx and others. Taylor, he argues, "sparked the revolution that allowed industrial workers to earn middle-class wages and achieve middle-class status despite their lack of skill and education."[2]

Alas, there is no Frederick Taylor equivalent for knowledge work. As a result we lack measures, methods, and rules of thumb for improvement. Some may breathe a sigh of relief at this, given that Taylor imposed a level of structure and discipline on manual labor that the laborers themselves often resented. However, I am not suggesting that the same approaches employed by Taylor would work for knowledge workers—in fact, they would be likely to lead to disaster. So there is no need to view this book—and other attempts to improve knowledge worker performance—as "a new Taylorism." [3]

With no clear alternative to Taylorist approaches, however, there may be attempts to apply those approaches to knowledge work. We have already seen such attempts in more structured, lower-level forms of knowledge work, such as call centers. There isn't even a need for Taylor's famous clipboard and stopwatch, for such workers are measured by the computers and software they employ in their jobs. This may have led to some improvements in the quantity of work—more calls per hour processed, for example—but you don't need to call many call centers to see what has happened to the quality of customer service.

What we need, then, are approaches to improving the performance of knowledge work that are neither simplistic nor mechanical, and that assess both the number and the quality of the distinctive outputs produced. We need to employ not only faster movement through the components of knowledge work, but also to allow for the reflection and creative thinking that knowledge workers require to be effective. We need not only to improve the work processes that knowledge workers use today, but to design entirely new processes that take advantage of the technologies that didn't exist even a decade ago.

What's the Objective for Knowledge Work Interventions?

It's becoming common for people to refer to or discuss "knowledge worker productivity," although I don't think this is the optimal objective. Productivity is a measure that is well-ensconced in the field of economics, and we receive monthly reports from our governments on the rise and fall of productivity. Economists have figured out ways (sometimes a bit dubious) to quantify productivity at the level of the overall economy, despite the difficulties of measuring knowledge work and services. Productivity is typically measured as outputs divided by the inputs necessary to produce them. At the aggregate level, economists measure outputs in terms of dollars produced by work, and inputs in terms of labor and capital. This approach works as a rough measure of aggregate economic performance at the national level.

It's not very useful, however, for actually improving knowledge work. First, productivity only indirectly addresses the quality of work, in that people are presumably willing to pay more for high-quality work than low. Quality is a critical factor in knowledge work, and it's usually not good enough to measure it by how much people will pay.

Second, it's often difficult with knowledge work to determine clearly what is an "output." As Charles Leadbeater, the British social commentator, has expressed it:

> Most people in most advanced economies produce nothing that can be weighed: communications, software, advertising, financial services. They trade, write, design, talk, spin and create: rarely do they make anything. The assets they work with are just as ephemeral as their output.[4]

So knowledge worker outputs are difficult to define and measure. If a strategic planner produces a brilliant strategic plan—but for some reason her organization never implements it—is that a successful output? If a manager decides to initiate a merger with another firm, is that decision an output?

Third, inputs in productivity analysis don't encompass all the factors that can affect the quality and quantity of outputs. Management approaches that make knowledge workers satisfied and happy may not cost any more than those that make them miserable, yet the different approaches will surely have an impact on these workers' outputs. Even information technology is not really assessed by productivity analysis—it's simply considered an aspect of overhead.

We won't eliminate productivity as a measure, but we do need to seek more from knowledge workers. I like terms such as "performance" and "results." They can encompass productivity *and* quality, efficiency, and effectiveness. They're not restricted by a narrow economist's definition. Whatever business process or activity a knowledge worker is trying to accomplish, we can define the level of performance and results for it in terms of speed, cost, freedom from defects, or customer satisfaction. Performance and results can be granular enough to employ as measures for individual knowledge workers, groups of them within organizations, or entire organizations. So while I will occasionally refer to productivity throughout this book, what I really think we should strive for is increased performance and better results.

Measurement

A key component of management has always been to evaluate the performance of workers. In the industrial age, this was a relatively easy task; an individual worker's productivity could be assessed through outputs—work actually produced—or visible inputs, including hours worked or apparent effort expended. One aspect of both the Taylorist and economic productivity approaches is that they allow for universal measures. Productivity-oriented approaches convert the value of outputs to currency. Taylorist approaches are generally oriented to the measurement of time. It is very appealing to look across an entire corporation or even a country and argue that we have increased productivity or performance by an exact percentage—however poor or meaningless those measures may actually be.

In the world of knowledge work, evaluating performance is much more difficult. How can a manager determine whether enough of a knowledge worker's brain cells are being devoted to a task? What's the formula for assessing the creativity and innovation of an idea? Given the difficulty of such evaluations, managers of knowledge workers have traditionally fallen back on measuring visible inputs, e.g., hours worked. Hence the long hours put in by attorneys, investment bankers, and consultants. However, the increasing movement of knowledge work out of the office and into homes, airplanes, and client sites makes it difficult to use hours worked as a measure, and that criterion never had much to do with the quality of knowledge produced.

Perhaps the greatest problem in measuring knowledge work deals with quality. By what criteria can we establish that one research paper, one advertising slogan, or one new chemical compound is better than another? If you can't easily measure the quality of knowledge work, it makes it difficult to determine who does it well, and what interventions might make it work better. Many organizations tend to fall back on measuring the volume of knowledge outputs produced—lines of programming code, for example—simply because it's possible to measure them. But without some measure of quality, the improvement of knowledge work is unlikely to go very well.

Fortunately, there is an answer to measuring the quality of knowledge work, although it's subjective. It involves determining a relevant peer group for the particular workers involved, and asking them what they think of the work. This technique has often been used, for example, in evaluating professors for promotion and tenure. A jury of peers—usually from within and outside the professor's school—is consulted, and the quality of the candidates' published work assessed. Similarly, student evaluations are used to assess the quality of teaching. Any problems with lack of objectivity are made up for by the volume of responses. In the same fashion, a few organizations ask for multiple peer evaluations in annual performance reviews and promotion decisions. Some knowledge management applications ask each user of the system to rate the quality of the knowledge found. Thus there are means of assessing quality, although the peer group and the assessment approach will vary according to context.

In general, I believe that we'll never get very far in improving the performance of knowledge work with a universal measure—either of quality or quantity of outputs. What matters is *high-quality* outputs per unit of time and cost, and the specific outputs vary widely across knowledge worker types. A computer programmer produces lines of code; a physician produces well people; a scientist produces discoveries and research papers. The only way we can determine whether a particular intervention improves knowledge work performance is to assess both the quantity and quality of the outputs produced by those workers. Universal measures are pretty much useless for this purpose.

Therefore, the appropriate measure for knowledge work will vary by industry, process, and job. If you're trying to improve knowledge worker performance, it's extremely important to determine what measures make sense for the work you're focusing on, and then to apply them. Organizations need to begin to employ a broad array of inputs and outputs, some of which are internal to the knowledge worker's mind. One input might involve the information and knowledge that a knowledge worker consulted in making a decision or taking an action (a particularly important criterion for managers). ABB, the global electrical and engineering firm, uses this factor as one of many in assessing managerial performance. Another input could be the process that a knowledge worker follows in producing knowledge work. The self-reported allocation of the knowledge worker's time and attention is a third possible input.[5]

Outputs could include the volume of knowledge produced, the quality of the decisions or actions taken on the basis of knowledge, and the impact of the knowledge produced (as judged by others). In the consulting business, some consultants are already evaluated in part on the knowledge they bring to the firm and the impact it has on clients—in addition to the usual measures of chargeability and consulting projects sold.

Output measures are, of course, the classical approach to evaluating processes. However, it's all too easy for organizations to refer vaguely to improved knowledge work performance without giving any specific measures or numerical targets. Many thousands of IT projects, for example, have been justified under the banner of "better information for improved decision making," with nary a measure or even a detailed look back at a single decision. All too many facilities changes have been rationalized under the name of "better communications," with no measurement of any communications-related variable. Even many companies' efforts to improve more operational and administrative processes have often lacked measurable goals, and given the difficulties of measuring knowledge work, we can expect measures to be lacking even more frequently.

Of course, some knowledge work processes are more easily measured than others. Information technology is certainly one of the better-off segments. There are two domains in which IT measurement is relatively advanced: programming, and IT processes and capabilities. In programming, some organizations have measured for decades the production of either lines of code or function points, and various researchers have analyzed the considerable variance in productivity. These measures aren't perfect, but they have allowed IT organizations to begin to understand differences across groups and individuals. How many times have you heard that the best programmer is ten times as productive as the worst? We may not know exactly how to bring everybody up to that high level, but we at least know the degree of variation—something that lawyers, doctors, and (executive) chiefs can't measure nearly as well. (By the way, one of my other favorite research findings is that programmers with bigger offices are more productive. Feel free to try that one out on your boss!)

The other primary domain of measurement is the assessment of IT processes and capabilities, particularly software engineering (but also software acquisition, people management, and the development of software-intensive products). Thanks to the Software Engineering Institute and researcher Watts Humphrey, we have an international standard for the quality of software engineering: the Capability Maturity Models.[6] You've probably heard of these five-level models, against which thousands of organizations have been assessed. CMMs have been enormously influential in the offshore movement of software development to places such as India and China. The fact that there are so many organizations certified at the top Level 5 CMM in India—more than twice as many as in the United States, unfortunately—has led many companies to send work offshore with confidence. The Software Engineering Institute has developed a more general approach to assessing capability maturity (called CMMI—Capability Maturity Model Integration), but thus far it has largely been applied to software-related processes only.[7]

Regrettably, there is no similar global standard for other forms of knowledge work capability, unless you count the ISO 9000 family of standards for manufacturing quality. Of course, the availability of a global standard cuts both ways. It means that knowledge work will flow to where it is best and most cheaply done, and that may well be outside your company or country. But it's also a great yardstick if you want to get better.

The CMM is a good example of a measure that assesses elements of quality, rather than just productivity (it actually assesses whether approaches are in place to measure and improve quality). Since the quality of knowledge work outputs is a particularly critical issue in overall performance, it's important to determine a means of measuring it. Knowledge creation activities are particularly problematic in this regard—how do we determine whether a new drug compound, a new strategic plan, or a new article are of high quality? In the long run, we can know whether the drug was introduced and sold well in the marketplace, and whether the article was cited by other scholars. In the short run, this is difficult to assess with precision. The only means of assessment are typically subjective—asking other people to assess quality. For an organization assessing the quality of an individual knowledge worker's contributions, it's important to solicit opinions from a wide variety of people, and to try to remove any sources of bias. If you are an individual knowledge worker, it's important to maintain a network of people who know and respect the quality of your work.

What Doesn't Work

In addition to applying inappropriate measures such as the clipboard-and-stopwatch approaches of Frederick Taylor, there are a variety of other dead-end interventions that will not improve knowledge work performance. Some of these have been tried and haven't worked. Some just don't make sense, but will undoubtedly be attempted by someone.

Top-down Reengineering

Top-down reengineering of knowledge work was attempted by some organizations in the mid-1990s when reengineering was popular. Most organizations had the good sense to realize that it wasn't a good idea to tell knowledge workers how to do their work without spending a great deal of time understanding it, but a few went ahead and did it anyway. They created detailed maps of processes, subprocesses, and sub-subprocesses, and released them in binders to those who did the work. This didn't cause a great deal of harm, because the knowledge workers generally ignored the new process flows. It just wasted a lot of money.

I saw this from a couple of perspectives—as a consultant and researcher to organizations that tried it (though I generally advised against it), and as an employee of a company that tried to do it to me. In both cases I found out that it's very difficult to impose a new process on a large group of knowledge workers who don't want to work that way. Too much of the work is invisible or is carried out in a way that it can't easily be assessed or measured.

Once, for example, I stopped by my office at a consulting firm on my way home from the airport. I found on my desk a new, colorful, shrink-wrapped binder entitled "The Management Consulting Process." I vaguely knew that a process reengineering project had been under way, but the most salient fact for me was that I had never been consulted about it—even though I had written the first book ever published on business process reengineering. Further adding to my distaste for this binder was my feeling, which most knowledge workers share, that my work was different from that of most of my colleagues at the firm. I was more a researcher and writer than a consultant, and felt that it was highly unlikely that my particular brand of consulting had been addressed in "The Management Consulting Process." So what did I do with this binder? I decided to be a good corporate citizen and not put it in the trashcan immediately. I simply put it on my bookshelf. On one slow day, I even browsed through a few pages. Eventually I threw it away when I left that particular firm. I should perhaps have studied it to make sure that it was irrelevant to my work, but I suspect that my reaction was typical even for "mainstream" consultants at the firm—all of whom probably considered themselves well out of the mainstream.

The lesson here is that almost all knowledge workers need to feel that they have participated in the design or redesign of their work if they are going to follow a new process. This can be logistically difficult to do if there are many workers involved in the same process. Representative democracy may be a viable alternative in some circumstances—if knowledge workers feel that peers whom they respect have been involved in the work, it may be enough to gain a level of compliance.

Scripting

The scripting of work has been a popular approach to improving performance at the lower, less-skilled levels of knowledge work. The assumption here is that an expert can lay out a script for lower-level knowledge workers that tells them what to say under certain circumstances, particularly in dealings with customers. This approach has been most prevalent in call centers—it's quite likely that call center representatives have read scripted sales pitches to you. Even at this low level of skill, scripting can be problematic. We know how it feels to be read to. Reading a script is not only often apparent to the customer, but it also ensures that the worker won't engage his or her full faculties and creativity in the job. It may bring the lowest performers up to a certain level of proficiency, but it is highly unlikely to create a high-performing knowledge workforce. And the higher the level of knowledge and skills required to do a job, the less likely that scripting will be of use at all.

Nonetheless, the use of scripting is growing, and is probably being used in many areas where it shouldn't be applied. For example, scripting is being used in some school districts—including the New York City schools—in order to teach primary school children to read. A series of *New York Times* articles on a new first-grade teacher in New York made it clear that teachers who followed the script were better rewarded than those who relied on the traditional teaching virtues—e.g., getting to know children and diagnosing their individual capabilities. I don't know about you, but I am just as glad that my first grade teacher didn't have a script to teach me how to read (somehow I managed to learn anyway).

Scripting has its place, and I will come back to it several times throughout this book—sometimes as a valid means of improving a knowledge-based process. For the most part, however, it's a lowest-common-denominator approach, and it's better to steer clear of it if you care about the quality of knowledge worker outputs.

Computer-Mediated Processes for Everyone

One of the things I will advocate in this book is that, when possible, it's a good idea to have computers mediate and structure the work of knowledge workers. The idea is that a computer brings work, information, and knowledge to the worker, and most significant actions that a knowledge worker takes would be entered into, or at least noted by, a computer. If you had to choose a single step to make knowledge work more productive and effective, this would probably be the one you should select. I will describe the many benefits and examples of this approach in chapter 5, where the entire topic is treated at length.

Yet it would be folly to presume that this is the answer to all problems of improving knowledge work and of all knowledge workers. Some of the drawbacks to computer-mediated work are the same ones that befall scripting (and scripts are often on computer screens): at times we should be paying attention not to computer screens, but to the voices and faces of human beings. I don't mind if my doctor occasionally glances at the computer during my brief time with him, but mostly I'd like him to be focusing on me and my symptoms.

Some of the other problems with computer-mediated work involve the structure they impose. The more creative knowledge work should not be highly-structured—by a computer, an overly controlling boss, or anything else. Humans are more innovative and insightful when they have the time to think and reflect, and it's typically not much help for a computer to be standing by with blank lines in a form and a blinking cursor.

Similarly, computers tend to impose time pressure on knowledge work. When a computer begins to structure and measure the flow of work, it's usually not very long before a manager attempts to speed it up. It doesn't have to be that way, but since it's all too easy to measure the time a task takes when that task is being performed on a computer, this sort of measurement often rears its ugly head. Theresa Amabile's work has documented the detrimental effects of time pressure on creativity, so if creativity is needed in a knowledge work process, you might want to keep highly-structured automation away from it.[8]

Treating All Knowledge Workers in the Same Way

This book is being written with the assumption that knowledge workers can be addressed as a group with regard to their work performance and interventions in it. Yet it would be a big mistake to treat all knowledge workers as if they were the same. In chapter 4, I will describe some of the different types of knowledge workers and the implications of those types. Suffice it to say here, however, that in some respects knowledge work is all over the map, and that you can make significant errors if you don't recognize the differences before attempting to intervene.

Some of the issues I've discussed in this chapter, for example, are much more relevant to some knowledge workers than others. Scripting works for some types of call center workers, but would be a disaster for a scientist. Computer-mediated work may be feasible for physicians in some health care settings, but not for those in others, or not for nurses.

Even top-down reengineering may be successful for some lower-level and relatively docile knowledge workers, though it is generally a bad idea. So even when I make broad, sweeping generalizations about knowledge workers, you have to temper them with the realization that all knowledge workers are hardly alike.

A Note on Experiments

We're in the early days of thinking and knowing about how to improve knowledge work. Obviously I feel that I know enough to write a book about the subject, but there is much more to be learned. Every attempt to make it better is—or should be—an experiment. Every time an organization employs a new technology, a new process flow, or a new design for workspace, it is experimenting with knowledge work improvement. And these experiments take place every day in the United States, Europe, Japan, and other sophisticated economies.

The problem is that we don't treat them as experiments. We adopt new ways of officing, organizing, and operating based not on rational experimentation and learning, but rather on faddish inclinations and gut feel. If other companies are moving to "hearths" in their offices and allowing workers to bring in pets, your company decides it's a good idea too. If your gadget-guru friend gets a combination PDA and cell phone, you want to check one out as well. If an office furniture maker comes out with a new line of cubicle furniture and assures buyers that it leads to enhanced communication, it gets bought—particularly if it takes up less square footage per worker than the previous office arrangement. Occasionally the benefits of intervening in knowledge work are converted into return on investment analyses in order to get funding, but few if any companies go back and measure what was really saved or gained.

Experiments involve rigor and discipline. Companies doing true experiments measure the salient aspects of the work environment both before and after they make a change. They only change one thing at a time so that they can isolate the reason for any improvement or detriment to the work. They remember what they learned from the experiment—perhaps even write it down! While there is increasing recognition that experimentation is important for innovation and strategy, this trend hasn't made a lot of headway into knowledge work. [9] However, a number of organizations are learning from their interventions in this area.

For example, Capital One, a leading credit card provider, is approaching this level of disciplined experimentation in its knowledge work improvement initiatives. It's natural that Capital One would undertake this type of internal experimentation, because it is known for its segmentation of its customer markets and its experimentation with different credit terms, direct marketing approaches, and customer incentives. For its own knowledge workers, the company is beginning a series of projects involving "Productivity and Knowledge Management" that are being overseen in a collaborative effort involving the Information Technology, Human Resources, and Corporate Real Estate functions. In one project, for example, Capital One is piloting an "Office of the Future" involving a variety of mobile technologies and a choice of several different open work environments. Over nine hundred workers are involved in the pilot, which is taking place in an entire building on its campus near Richmond, Virginia. The managers overseeing the pilot are developing measures and attitudinal surveys that will allow them to determine the business value of the experiment. Other projects involve a corporate portal and knowledge repository, and segmentation of workers into nonmobile, mobile, and telework categories.

Summary

Knowledge work interventions aren't science, and there is no need for total devotion to the scientific method in these experiments. But whatever type of intervention you undertake, it's worth spending some time and effort thinking about what you will learn from it. Can you treat the project as a pilot, implementing it in only part of the organization for a brief time, so you can see how the experimental subjects relate to the control group for which no change is made? Can you implement one idea at a time so that you can observe its effects, rather than changing everything at once? Results, not research, are the goal of knowledge work interventions. It's just difficult to know whether your intervention made any difference if there is a total absence of experimental discipline.

In this chapter I've described some of the "meta-issues" of knowledge work interventions: why to intervene in the first place, the objectives of intervention, how to measure knowledge work, and some common mistakes to avoid in knowledge work projects. In addition to earlier chapters on similarities and differences across knowledge workers, these discussions should be useful background for any effort to improve results from knowledge work. The remaining chapters of this book will address specific approaches to intervention. Chapter 4 will focus on how organizations can take a process orientation to knowledge work.

Recommendations for Getting Results from Knowledge Workers

- A laissez-faire approach to knowledge work won't lead to improved performance and results.

- There's no single performance measure for knowledge work; organizations need to determine what measures make sense for each individual situation.

- Top-down reengineering of knowledge work is unlikely to be successful.

- Scripting or having a computer tell workers what to do and say in their work may apply to low-level knowledge work jobs, but it is of limited value in more complex and integrated knowledge work processes.

- Computers can be helpful in improving knowledge work, but not all jobs can be mediated by a computer because they are too unstructured or collaborative in nature.

- Knowledge work performance improvement is an experiment, but most organizations aren't sufficiently disciplined in how they set up and measure the results of their experiments.

Knowledge Work Processes

A time-honored way of improving any form of work is to treat it as a process. To treat something as a process is to impose a formal structure on it—to identify its beginning, end, and intermediate steps, to clarify who the customer is for it, to measure it, to take stock of how well it is currently being performed, and ultimately to improve it. A process orientation implies design—we're not just accepting work the way it is, but trying to find better ways to perform it. Once this structure is imposed on work, the objectives for improvement may be incremental or radical, and there are various ways to improve processes. It is often a good idea to conduct a process analysis before applying technology to work, so that you don't automate a bad process. This process-based approach to improving performance is very familiar, and it's an obvious candidate for improving knowledge work activities.

But as I mentioned in chapter 3, knowledge workers haven't often been subject to this sort of analysis. In some cases they have actively avoided it, and in others it has just slid by them. I've noted that knowledge workers often have the power to resist being told what to do, and process analysis is usually a sophisticated approach to having someone else tell you how to do your job. It's also not easy to view knowledge work in process terms because much of it takes place in people's heads and because it's often collaborative and iterative, which makes it difficult to structure. When I've talked to knowledge workers about their jobs, they've often said that they don't think that their workdays are consistent and repeatable enough to be viewed as processes. This doesn't mean, of course, that a process perspective couldn't be applied, or that there couldn't be more structure to knowledge work jobs—only that there hasn't been thus far.

Knowledge workers are also subject to the same fallacy that manual workers have long been subjected to—the "work harder" approach. When faced with a need for better performance and results, many organizations and managers simply tell their workers of all types to work harder, rather than to work smarter. They may, as Nelson Repenning and John Sterman point out in a very thoughtful article, even cancel attempts to improve processes with the rationale that they are a waste of time.[1] This leads to a spiral of doom—knowledge workers work harder and harder (often taking their work home with them at night), but the process doesn't improve because there is no time to examine and change it. Process improvement, on the other hand, can lead to a virtuous cycle after some initial investment.

The more recent "knowledge management" movement, in which companies have attempted to capture and distribute knowledge in electronic form, hasn't helped much with regard to knowledge work processes either. Although I'm a big supporter of the idea and have written a couple of books on it, knowledge management activities have too often been imposed on top of existing work processes, and not altogether successfully. Few knowledge workers have any spare time today for recording their most recently learned lessons, or for taking calls from coworkers seeking their expertise. If we want knowledge workers to adopt these knowledge behaviors, we will have to free up some time for them to do so. The desired behaviors—creating, sharing, and using knowledge—will have to be "baked into" the job, and unnecessary activities eliminated.

Given the historical antipathy of knowledge workers to formalized processes, it's obvious that they will ask how a process orientation is in their interest. Many knowledge workers will view a formal process approach as a bureaucratic, procedural annoyance. A much more appealing possibility is that a process orientation will be beneficial to knowledge workers—that they will benefit from the discipline and structure that a process brings, while remaining free to be creative and improvisational when this is necessary and desirable. Whether this is true, of course, varies by the process involved, the way a process is implemented and managed, and the particular individuals involved.

There is some cause for optimism in this regard, however. Paul Adler, an organizational behavior researcher at USC, has studied the issue of what happens to one type of knowledge worker—software developers—as process orientation increases. In that particular process domain, there is a widely used measure of process orientation, the Software Engineering Institute's Capability Maturity Model (CMM), that allows analysis of different levels of process maturity. Adler looked at two groups within a company (Computer Sciences Corporation) that were at CMM Level 5, the highest level of process maturity, and two other groups in the same firm at Level 3.

Adler found that, for the most part, software developers experienced the increased process orientation as positive. Some comments from his paper are important for this question:

> ... the more routine tasks in software development were rendered more efficient by standardization and formalization, leaving the non-routine tasks relatively unstructured to allow more creativity in their performance.

> ... process maturity was experienced by many developers as enabling and empowering rather than coercive and alienating.

> Process maturity did mean a loss of autonomy. Higher CMM levels drew people into broader and tighter webs of interdependence . . .

> The key to ensuring a positive response to process discipline was extensive participation . . . People support what they help create.

This is good news for anyone interested in taking a process perspective on knowledge work. Of course, the findings aren't necessarily generalizable to all knowledge work, and much more research is needed. But it is a signal that a process orientation can make knowledge work more productive as well as "enabling and empowering" if managed correctly (i.e., with extensive participation).

There will probably also be cases in which knowledge workers actively resist or ignore a process orientation. In these cases, imposing it becomes a power struggle. The outcome of such struggles will vary across situations, but they won't be typical "management versus labor" conflicts. There won't be a typical union, for one thing—knowledge workers are rarely represented by a union, though they may be represented by a professional association. And knowledge workers are likely to use the language of quality and service to customers rather than the wages and hours issues that typically emerge in labor disputes. But there will be some battles, because adopting more effective and productive processes in many industries is likely to conflict with knowledge worker autonomy. As one expert (himself a doctor) in the health care industry, for example, puts it, "Less discretion for doctors would improve public safety."[2] Other industries are likely to face similar trade-offs.

Processes and Knowledge Work
Segments—That Matrix Again

As I've argued throughout this book, all knowledge workers aren't alike, and there are some key differences in process orientations among different types of knowledge work and workers. Recall again, for example, the four-cell matrix (figure 2-1) I introduced in chapter 2. Transaction work is generally more easily structured in process terms than any other, because the work is normally repeatable, and because the people who do the work have less discretion to do it the way they like. At the opposite extreme are collaboration workers, who generally represent a nightmare for process-oriented managers. These workers typically have an iterative, collaborative approach to work in which patterns are more difficult to discern. They may deny that their work has any structure at all—"every day is different," they've often said to me. And if you should figure out a process to recommend to these workers, they have the power and the independence to successfully resist it.

Integration and expert workers are somewhere in the middle in this process-orientation continuum. Integration work is often fairly structured, although higher levels of collaboration often lead to more process complexity. Integration-oriented workers are relatively likely to adopt process interventions. Expert work can be made more process-oriented, but experts themselves are a bit tricky. Typically one has to give them the ability to override or step out of the process, and they are often wary of "cookbook" approaches to their work.

Of course, it's not a binary question whether a process orientation is relevant to a particular type of knowledge work. For each of these types, I can provide some rules of thumb about how best to move in a more process-oriented direction:

- *Transaction workers:* These workers need to understand the flow of their work and the knowledge needed to perform it, but they rarely have time to consult external guidelines or knowledge sources. Fortunately, it's often relatively easy to embed a process flow into some form of computer-based application. These typically involve structured workflows or scripts. Such systems usually bring the work—and all information and knowledge required to perform it—to the worker, and they measure the process and worker productivity at the same time. It's not necessarily fun to have your job structured by a workflow system, but it is efficient.

- *Integration workers:* With this type of work, it's possible to articulate the process to be followed in documents, and workers typically have enough time and discretion to consult the documents. There is nothing new about describing a process, but the practice continues across many industries. Medical technicians, for example, often follow health care protocols in administering tests and treatments. Salespeople at the electronics retailer Best Buy follow a series of "standard operating procedures" for working with customers and making a sale. Even the U.S. Army describes in detail its "doctrine" for how work is done—and with new technologies and warfighting methods, that work is increasingly knowledge-oriented.

- *Expert workers:* These workers have high autonomy and discretion in their work, but there are some examples of organizations, such as Partners HealthCare and the VA hospitals, that have applied technology to key aspects of the process (in these cases, ordering medications, tests, referrals, and other medical actions). But unless there is a way to embed a computer into the middle of the work process, experts will be a challenge from the standpoint of structuring work. Instead of specifying detailed aspects of the work flow, those who attempt to improve expert knowledge work should provide templates, sample outputs, and high-level guidelines. It's unlikely that expert workers will pay much attention to detailed process flows anyway.

- *Collaboration workers:* As I've mentioned, this is the most difficult category to address in traditional process terms. The cautions noted above for experts also apply to collaborators—a gentle process touch is desirable. Specifying and measuring outputs, instilling a customer orientation, and fostering a sense of urgency are more likely to be successful intervention approaches than issuing process flow charts. If external knowledge and information are necessary to do the job, they must generally be made available through repositories and documents—it's very unusual for work in this category to be fully mediated and structured by a computer. Of course, this means that it's relatively less likely that the knowledge and information will be used.

Knowledge Creation, Distribution, and Application

The four types of knowledge work I've discussed above are not the only way to segment it in terms of processes. Perhaps a more obvious segmentation approach is to think about processes in terms of the knowledge activity involved. I discussed several such categories of activity in chapter 2—finding, creating, packaging, distributing, or applying knowledge. For purposes of thinking about process interventions, however, I'll use a simpler categorization—that is, the process orientation differs by whether workers create, distribute, or apply knowledge.[3] This simple three-step model—a process in itself—is a useful way to think about how different knowledge activities require different process interventions.

Creation

The bugaboo of process management is knowledge *creation*. This is widely viewed as an idiosyncratic, "black box" activity that is difficult if not impossible to manage as a process. I'll grant you difficult, but not impossible. Perhaps there are circumstances in which knowledge creation is totally unstructured, unmeasured, and unrepeatable—but in most situations I'd argue that progress can be made in the direction of process orientation.

One common approach to knowledge creation processes is simply to break them up into several pieces or stages. Many companies in the 1980s and '90s, for example, divided their new product development processes into a series of stages or phases. The objective was to allow evaluation of the new knowledge created at the transition from one stage to another—stage gates. A new drug compound, a new car design, or a new toy model would move through a stage gate if it met the criteria for moving ahead—typically a combination of technical and market feasibility factors. If this approach is employed in a disciplined fashion, it has the virtue of freeing up resources from unproductive projects without imposing too heavy a process burden on new product developers. However, this approach does not really address the activities within the stages, or treat the new product development activity as an end-to-end process.[4]

Other knowledge creation processes have been the subject of alternative approaches, but still with a relatively low degree of process orientation. Scientific research, for example, is the prototypical example of an unstructured knowledge creation process. While there are valid aspects of scientific research that are difficult to structure—the step made infamous in a *New Yorker* cartoon as "and then a miracle occurs"—there are plenty of approaches and tactics for bringing more process discipline to research. One is simply to measure outputs—number of patents or compounds or published papers per researcher per year, for example. Another is to assess quality—the number of citations a researcher receives per year, for example, is a widely used measure of scientific influence. A third approach is to involve customers of the research (either internal or external to the organization) in the creation process, so that their influence is more directly felt. A number of corporate research laboratories—including IBM's Watson Research Center and GE's Corporate Research & Development organization—have adopted this approach over the past several years as they attempt to become more productive and profitable. If an organization is creative—and doesn't automatically resort to process flowcharts—there are a number of ways to make knowledge creation processes more effective and efficient.

Another knowledge creation process is oil exploration. Geologists and geological engineers create seismological knowledge of a targeted drilling area, and try to progressively lower the risk of a dry hole with more knowledge over time. At Amerada Hess, a medium-sized oil firm with many exploration projects scattered around the globe, an attempt was made to map the process of oil exploration—the "Exploration Decision-Making Process." This was a cultural stretch for Hess, in that exploration had historically been a highly unstructured and iterative activity, and the people who did it enjoyed a free-thinking, "maverick" culture. Certainly there were benefits from the exercise; depicting the Exploration Decision-Making Process in a visual format greatly enhanced the ability of participants to understand their roles, responsibilities, and interactions throughout the process. But the process map got only mixed support from exploration managers. Simply documenting the history of each exploration prospect was a more successful intervention. The "Prospect Evaluation Sheet" reviewed the story and history of how the lead progressed to its current prospect level. This documentation served to encourage open discussions among peers of alternative interpretations and enabled them to make sense of ambiguities. Even more important was the insistence that peer reviews and peer assists take place before prospects could qualify to pass through decision gates. The Prospect Evaluation Sheet was just a way of recording how a prospect was maturing through the process.

In general, it seems that workers engaged in knowledge creation should be given some structure, but not too much. IDEO, the highly successful product design firm, for example, provides its employees with a structured brainstorming process, but few other processes have much if any structure or formality. Corning's R&D lab, like many scientific research organizations, employs a "stage gate" model of the innovation process, but there is substantial freedom within stages. More structure than these organizations provide would begin to seem heavy-handed.

Distribution

As for knowledge *distribution*—sharing or transfer are other words for this activity—it's also difficult to structure. Some professions, such as customer service, journalism, and library services, are only about distribution. For most knowledge workers, however, this is a part of the job, but not all of it. The lawyer or consultant is primarily responsible for generating solutions for clients, but also for sharing that solution with colleagues and searching out whether existing knowledge is already available that would help the client. The sharing of knowledge is difficult to enforce, since we don't know what any person knows, or how diligently he or she has searched for available knowledge. Yet there is a substantial body of research suggesting that knowledge worker groups that share knowledge perform better than those that do not.[5]

The most viable approach to managing knowledge distribution or sharing is not to manage the process itself, but rather the external circumstances in which knowledge distribution is undertaken. This typically involves changing where and with whom people work. Chrysler, for example, formed "platform teams" to improve the circulation of new car development knowledge across all the functions involved in building a car. Managers specified a process that instructed these teams to share knowledge at various points, but far more knowledge sharing occurred as a result of the platform teams' being put together in the same sections of Chrysler's Auburn Hills, Michigan, Technical Center.

Measurement is another reasonable tactic for improving knowledge distribution processes. It's easy to measure inputs (number of items contributed to repositories, number of participants in knowledge-sharing communities, etc.), but more challenging to measure what really matters (i.e., outputs and business value). Many organizations did cursory measurement of knowledge distribution in the early days of knowledge management, but never got beyond inputs.

Truly measuring the outputs of knowledge distribution activities, however, requires measuring improvements in the business processes involved. A customer service process in an IT firm, for example, distributes knowledge to customers. If you want to improve that knowledge distribution process, you have to identify key measures of process performance for customer service (such as the mean time it takes to solve a customer's problem, or the mean level of customer satisfaction with the result) and see how knowledge sharing improves those measures. Process performance measures can then often be translated into financial improvements.

Application

Then there is the application of knowledge, which is filtered through the human brain and applied to job tasks. Examples of this type of work include sales, computer programming, accounting, medicine, engineering, and most professions. All of these jobs involve a degree of knowledge creation, but that's not the primary objective—we generally want these knowledge workers not to invent new knowledge, but to apply existing knowledge in familiar or unfamiliar situations. We don't want computer programmers to create new programming languages, but rather to use existing ones to program applications. At best we want "small ideas" from these individuals—not reinvention of their jobs and companies.

How do we make knowledge application better? In many cases the goal is to reuse knowledge more effectively. We can greatly improve performance by having a lawyer reuse knowledge created in another case, or having a programmer employ a subroutine that someone else created. Knowledge asset reuse is a frequently stated objective for organizations, but it's hard to achieve. Many organizational and professional cultures reward—sometimes unconsciously—knowledge creation over knowledge reuse. Furthermore, effective reuse of knowledge asset requires investment in making knowledge reusable: documentation, libraries, catalogs, modular structures for knowledge objects. Many organizations and managers just don't take a sufficiently long view of reuse processes to make those investments.

When some colleagues and I researched knowledge asset reuse processes across several types of organizations, there were several factors explaining whether organizations were successful with reuse.[6] *Leadership* was one of the factors—having an executive in charge who understood the value of reuse and was willing to manage and invest so as to make reuse a reality. Another factor was *asset visibility*, or the ability to easily find and employ the knowledge asset when there was a desire to do so. The third and final factor was *asset control*, or the activities designed to ensure that the quality of knowledge assets was maintained over time. Therefore, anyone interested in knowledge reuse as a means of improving knowledge use processes must try to put these three factors in place.

There are other factors that can be employed to improve use. Computers, of course, can oversee the process of reuse. At GM's Vehicle Engineering Centers, for example new car designers are encouraged to reuse knowledge and engineering designs when possible, rather than create new ones. So the desirable dimensions of new vehicles and the parameters of existing component designs are programmed into the computer-aided design systems, and it becomes difficult for the engineers not to use them. One GM executive told me that you can't force the engineers to reuse designs and components—you just have to make it much easier for them to do that than to create new ones.

Today in most organizations, reuse is addressed only at the institutional level, if at all. But it stands to reason that the most effective knowledge workers reuse their own knowledge all the time. If I'm productive as an author, as I write this book I should be able to easily find and reuse previous passages I've written on the subject, perhaps with slightly different language to avoid plagiarizing myself and my publishers (I won't comment on how well I actually do this). A productive lawyer would index and rapidly find all the opinions and briefs he's ever written, and routinely reuse them for new clients. But while we know this is true, organizations have yet to help knowledge workers execute this sort of reuse. If they were smart, they'd make it easier—and would also provide taxonomies, training, role models, and encouragement.

Breaking the Process into Stages

One final way to think about knowledge work processes is to subdivide them into their constituent stages. Some stages of a process are more amenable to structuring and active intervention than others. For example, it's not for nothing that the early stages of the new product development process are often called the "fuzzy front end." At this point it's not clear what the customer requirements are, what the new product should do, or how it will work. There are things that can be done to make the fuzzy front end somewhat less fuzzy (*quality function deployment*, for example, is a method for clearly articulating customer requirements; *conjoint analysis* is a statistical technique used to calculate the relative value of different product attributes to customers). However, no amount of technique or process management is going to make the fuzzy front end as clear and well-structured as the final stages of new product development (e.g., manufacturing or market testing). Therefore, it makes sense to apply different interventions to the beginning of the process than to the end based on the inherent degree of structure in each stage.

There may be other factors that make particular stages more amenable to process thinking. Suppose, for example, that I'm trying to improve the consulting process. I could focus on marketing and sales activities, which are primarily done by senior partners, and involve lots of iterative back-and-forth negotiations with the client. Or I could address the process by which the work actually gets done for the client in a consulting project. Much more of this work is done by lower-level associates, whose behaviors might be a bit easier to influence. The overall nature of the work at this stage has also already been agreed upon by the client and the firm, so it is already more structured. If it were my job to improve this process, I'd use traditional process techniques on the latter stage, but not on the marketing and sales subprocess. They shouldn't be ignored, but they require different—and a bit more subtle—techniques.

Process Versus Practice in Knowledge Work

After spending several pages talking about taking a process perspective on knowledge work, let me temper this message a bit. It's important to remember that there is also a *practice* side to knowledge work, which has to be balanced with the process perspective.

I believe that if we're going to succeed in making knowledge work processes better we have to grasp this key distinction (it will also help us with other types of processes, but it's absolutely essential for knowledge work). I first became aware of the difference after reading an important article called "Organizational Learning and Communities of Practice" by John Seely Brown and Paul Duguid in a somewhat obscure academic journal.[7] After reading this truly seminal piece, I recognized my own process-oriented biases, and became a convert to combining process and practice ever since.[8]

Every effort to change how work is done needs a dose of both *process*—the design for how work is to be done—and *practice*, an understanding of how individual workers respond to the real world of work and accomplish their assigned tasks. Process work is a design, modeling, and engineering activity, sometimes created by teams of analysts or consultants who don't actually do the work in question and who often have only a dim understanding of how it's being done today

(I am entitled to say this, because I've committed this sort of error myself). A process design is fundamentally an abstraction of how work should be done in the future. Process analysts may superficially address the "as is" process, but generally only as a quick preamble to the "to be" environment. Those with a strong process orientation to knowledge work are implying, "I know you think for a living. But I can think better about your own living than you can."

Practice analysis is more like anthropology—it's a well-informed description of how work is done today by those who actually do it. Some analyses of work practice are done by certified anthropologists (ethnographers), who observe workers carefully over a period of months, either through participant observation or through video. To really understand work practice requires detailed observation and a philosophical acceptance that there are usually good reasons for why work gets done by workers in a particular way. Just the acceptance of the practice idea suggests a respect for workers and their work, and an acknowledgement that they know what they're doing much of the time.

A pure focus on process in knowledge work means that a new design is unlikely to be implemented successfully; it probably won't be realistic. We've all seen examples of new process designs or models that don't have a chance of working in the real world. On the other hand, a pure focus on practice isn't very helpful either—it leads to a great description of today's work activities, but it may not improve them much. Some anthropologists go just as far in the practice direction as some consultants go in the process direction. They argue that you have to observe work for a year or so in order to have any chance of understanding it at all, which is clearly unrealistic in a business context.

To successfully change knowledge work you've got to have a delicate interplay of process and practice. It's certainly true that some processes can be designed by outsiders and implemented successfully—because they're relatively straightforward to begin with or because it's easy to use people or systems to structure and monitor their performance.

Other jobs—particularly those involving knowledge, discretion, and outside interventions from groups like customers or business partners—are very difficult for outsiders to understand and design, and require a high proportion of practice orientation.

The worst offenders among purveyors of process management have tried to make the design of all new processes a real engineering discipline. They focus heavily, for example, on the modeling language used to describe a business process, and less on what really happens in it. Some want to model a process quickly, and then automatically generate program code from the model to build the information system to support the process. Others describe in excruciating detail the most rational way to design a "best practice" process—again, with little understanding of why work is done the way that it is.

One might occasionally get away with this sort of thing when the process is performed by low-level, less educated, inarticulate workers. But try this with knowledge workers and you'll be put in your place. They know all the reasons a new process design won't work, and they're articulate enough to describe those reasons to executives. And getting them angry is a big mistake, since they hold the organization's future in their heads.

What does it mean to combine a process and practice orientation? Here are some obvious implications:

- Involve the knowledge workers in the design of the new process. Ask them what they'd like to see changed and what's stopping them from being more effective and efficient.

- Watch them do their work (not for a year, but a few weeks isn't unreasonable). Take your time. Devote as much attention to the "as is" as the "to be." Knowledge work is invisible, and it takes a while to understand the flow, rationale, and variations of the work process.

- Talk to knowledge workers about why they do the things they do. Don't automatically assume that you know a better way.

- Enlist analysts who have actually done the work in question. If you're trying to improve health care processes, for example, use doctors and nurses to design the new process.

- Exercise some deference. Treat experienced workers as real experts (they probably are!). Get them on your side with credible assurances that your goal is to make their lives better.

- Use the Golden Rule of Process Management. Ask yourself, "Would I want to have my job analyzed and redesigned in the fashion that I'm doing it to others?"

Types of Process Interventions

There are many different types of process-oriented interventions that we can make with knowledge work. Process improvement can be radical or incremental; participative or top-down; one-time or continuous; focused on large, cross-functional processes or on small ones at the work group level; and oriented to process flows or other attributes of processes. There's no single right answer to the question of which variant makes sense—it obviously depends on the organization's strategy, the degree of improvement necessary, and the type of work.

However, as I've noted, with knowledge work it's a good idea to make the improvement process as participative as possible. Knowledge workers are much more likely to agree with and adopt process changes if they have taken an active role in designing them. This begins to restrict the change options somewhat. It's very difficult to have thousands of people providing input in a highly participative change approach, so that largely dictates a focus on small processes. And because it's somewhat difficult for large numbers of people who are highly conversant with a process to develop a radical new approach to performing it, participative change also typically yields more incremental change results. Participative, incremental change processes are often also continuous, as opposed to one-time, in their orientation. It doesn't make sense to make one-time incremental changes if the organization isn't going to follow them up with more improvements over time.

The most common forms of process intervention for knowledge work, then, are participative, incremental, and continuous. One example of this type of approach in practice would be Six Sigma, which has been adapted and adopted for knowledge work by a variety of firms. General Electric, for instance, uses it extensively within its Global Research organization. It applies Six Sigma in research and design processes using its "Design for Six Sigma" (DFSS) methodology, which is about understanding the effects of variation on product performance before the product is actually manufactured. Many GE researchers and engineers have Six Sigma green or black belts and are experts in the application of statistical analysis to research and engineering processes, making the company perhaps the most advanced of all organizations in applying process management techniques to research.

The other key aspect of selecting a process-oriented intervention is the particular attribute of process management an organization addresses. As I've mentioned, it's all too common for organizations to interpret a "process" as a "flow diagram" that specifies "first you do this, and then you do this . . ." Such an engineering orientation to processes breaks down work into a series of sequential steps, and it's the aspect of process management that knowledge workers like least. Forms of this orientation appear when organizations attempt to create detailed methodologies for knowledge work, such as a system development methodology. It may be necessary in some cases to engineer the process flow, but it shouldn't be the centerpiece of a knowledge work improvement initiative.

So what's the alternative? There are many. I've discussed measures, identifying a customer for the process, and manipulating where and with whom knowledge workers do their work (to be described in much greater detail in chapter 8). In terms of documents, I've briefly mentioned the "tools and templates" approach to processes, which gives knowledge workers some examples and illustrations of what to do without beating them over the head with process flow and detailed methods.

Let me give you an example. I've already described my problem with the big binder, "The Management Consulting Process," that showed up on my desk one day. It carefully specified every step in the process, with glorious four-color flow diagrams. It seemed too rigid and structured, and neither I nor any of the people I respected in the firm had participated in creating it, so I ignored it.

This same firm (Ernst & Young), however, learned its lesson. Just as I was leaving it, I participated in the creation of the first "Power-pack"—a toolkit on how to propose projects to clients on improving their order management processes. The goal was to speed up the process of creating proposals for clients. According to the firm's Web site (ten years later), Powerpacks are still going strong and are described thus:

> It's a compilation of outstanding proposals, presentations, competitive information, models, specialized tools, and a variety of other relevant business resources. In other words, a Powerpack contains the "best of the best" information Ernst & Young offers, which is available to employees electronically.[9]

In my day, Powerpacks were available only in binder or CD form, but they were still very popular. They gave consultants all the tools they needed to be successful and productive but didn't tell them how to use the materials, and didn't make them feel like automatons. Because each Powerpack described a specific client problem, they weren't terribly unwieldy.

This "softer" approach of using tools and templates is only one alternative to highly engineered processes. Others might be called "agile" methods. They are less focused on the specific steps to be followed in a process and more oriented toward the managerial and cultural context surrounding the process. Instead of detailed process flows, for example, agile methods might emphasize the size and composition of process teams, a highly iterative work flow, and a culture of urgency. As yet these are only established within software development, but I suspect that over time they will migrate to other knowledge work processes.

Martin Fowler, an expert on agile methods, describes the contrast between engineered methodologies and agile approaches in common-sense language on his Web site:

> Methodologies impose a disciplined process upon software development with the aim of making software development more predictable and more efficient. They do this by developing a detailed process with a strong emphasis on planning inspired by other engineering disciplines—which is why I tend to refer to them as *engineering methodologies*.
>
> Engineering methodologies have been around for a long time. They've not been noticeable for being terribly successful. They are even less noted for being popular. The most frequent criticism of these methodologies is that they are bureaucratic. There's so much stuff to do to follow the methodology that the whole pace of development slows down.
>
> As a reaction to these methodologies, a new group of methodologies have appeared in the last few years. For a while these were known as lightweight methodologies, but now the accepted term is *agile methodologies*. For many people the appeal of these agile methodologies is their reaction to the bureaucracy of the monumental methodologies. These new methods attempt a useful compromise between no process and too much process, providing just enough process to gain a reasonable payoff . . . [Two key differences between adaptive and engineering methods are:]

- *Agile methods are adaptive rather than predictive.* Engineering methods tend to try to plan out a large part of the software process in great detail for a long span of time—this works well until things change. So their nature is to resist change. The agile methods, however, welcome change. They try to be processes that adapt and thrive on change, even to the point of changing themselves.

- *Agile methods are people-oriented rather than process-oriented.* The goal of engineering methods is to define a process that will work well whoever happens to be using it. Agile methods assert that no process will ever make up for the skill of the development team, so the role of a process is to support the development team in their work.[10]

One of the agile methods for software development that Fowler describes is known as "extreme programming," which emphasizes small teams, iterative development, frequent testing, and rapid outputs. There are several other agile approaches to software development that have somewhat different attributes, but they are all more flexible and people-focused than the detailed engineering approaches to software that were frequently proposed in the 1970s and '80s. It's not hard to imagine that before long we'll see analogues in other knowledge work process domains, such as "extreme product development."

Summary

In this chapter I've talked about process-oriented approaches to improving knowledge work, covering the issues of measures, different types of knowledge work processes, and alternatives to process engineering. I've pointed out that a process approach, rather than being the only way to improve a knowledge worker's performance (as some believe), is only one of many possible approaches. I've also demonstrated that the engineering perspective on processes has to be balanced against the day-to-day practice of knowledge workers, and have described some of the "softer" means of intervening into knowledge work.

In an ideal situation, knowledge work processes can create a climate in which innovation and discipline coexist. Knowledge workers are often passionate about their ideas, and won't abandon them easily. Yet it is sometimes necessary to kill some knowledge work initiatives in order to free up resources for new ones. Managers in pharmaceutical firms, for example, have noted that a key aspect of a strong drug development program is the ability to cancel projects that don't meet success criteria. But cancellation should be the result of a process, not a matter of an individual's taste.

Kao Corporation, Japan's largest consumer products firm, is an example of an organization with both a strong orientation to knowledge and learning, and a sense of process-oriented discipline when necessary. Kao's CEO talks about the company as an "educational institution," and it was one of the earliest adopters of knowledge management in Japan. Kao's researchers have a high degree of autonomy in the research they pursue, at least for Japanese firms. But Kao also has discipline. It has well-structured continuous process improvement programs, even in the R&D function. It also kills undesirable products and projects when necessary. In one striking example, the company had entered the floppy disk business and had become the world's second largest producer, but by the late 1990s it became clear that the business was fully commoditized. Most large Japanese firms are slow to restructure, but Kao quickly closed down first half, and then all, of the floppy disk business. The year 1998 was the first in seventeen that Kao had not grown profits, but it was already back on the profit growth track by 1999—and it's continued on that track since then.

Organizations like Kao take a process approach to knowledge work because it has been proven to be successful. Among the approaches to knowledge work improvement, a process approach is among the most disciplined, structured, and analytical. In chapter 5 we're going to discuss how information technologies can augment organizational processes for knowledge work.

Recommendations for Getting Results from Knowledge Workers

- Viewing knowledge work as a process can be an effective way to improve performance, although one must take care not to rely exclusively on the process perspective for this type of work.

- There is some evidence that taking more of a process orientation to their work can be somewhat liberating for knowledge workers, because they can concentrate on the more creative and unstructured aspects of their jobs.

- With knowledge work it's a good idea to make the improvement process as participative as possible. Knowledge workers are much more likely to agree with and adopt any process changes if they have been a party to designing them.

- Process-oriented interventions should vary by the type of knowledge work being addressed; more transaction-oriented work is the most amenable to the use of traditional process flow diagrams, for example. Process approaches should also differ by whether knowledge is being created, distributed, or applied in the work process.

- The most common forms of process intervention for knowledge work are participative, incremental, and continuous; Six Sigma is one good example of such an intervention.

- "Agile" methods and techniques for governing and improving work processes are typically better than "engineering" methods where knowledge work is concerned.

Organizational Technology for Knowledge Workers

Technology has been perhaps the single most important intervention in knowledge worker performance over the past couple of decades. The advent of personal computers, personal productivity software, personal digital assistants, mobile technologies, and other applications for the support of knowledge work has transformed it considerably. Knowledge workers can now create, share, and use information and knowledge almost anywhere and at any time. It is safe to assume that few knowledge workers would give up these capabilities.

Still, it is not necessarily safe to assume that these technologies have always enhanced knowledge worker productivity. We know that we've spent a lot on new technologies, and we know that productivity overall in the economy has risen. But we know very little about how knowledge workers actually use these technologies, and how their jobs have been affected. There are obvious benefits, such as the ability to edit documents without retyping them, or the ability to make small changes in a spreadsheet-based financial plan without fully recreating it. But there are obvious problems as well—lack of reliability, too much time spent fussing with equipment and applications and functions, e-mail spam, and so forth.

As I write these words, for example, I've just wasted fifteen minutes trying to connect to a wireless network in the Frankfurt airport. Time was wasted with not only one mobile device—my laptop—but two: the wireless vendor claims to have sent my password in a message to my mobile phone, which doesn't work in this airport. Could I get a phone that did work in Germany? Yes, but that would take more time. I'll probably waste even more time getting the credit card charge removed from my account, assuming I remember to do that. No aspect of this saga will surprise the mobile knowledge worker, who has undoubtedly wasted vast amounts of time in similar circumstances.

Technology to support knowledge workers can operate at two different levels. In this chapter I'll describe technologies that operate at the organizational level, supporting large numbers of workers doing the work of their companies. The other type supports individual workers, and I will describe these technologies in chapter 6. For the most part I will describe the positive implications of technology for knowledge worker performance, but keep in mind that the dark side—lost productivity and frustration—is always lurking in the background!

The Application That Fits the Role

Knowledge workers have different types of jobs, and thus it is obviously not appropriate to use the same technologies for all knowledge work. The matrix I introduced in chapter 2 is a useful foundation for thinking about the types of technologies that make sense for any particular type of knowledge work; figure 5-1 shows where some of these technologies can be applied within the matrix.[1] In the transaction cell,

FIGURE 5-1

Organizational technologies for different types of knowledge work

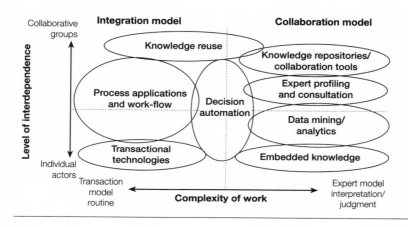

where work involves relatively low amounts of collaboration and judgment, the most appropriate technologies are those that automate structured transactions. A call center system that brings calls and the relevant information and knowledge to the worker would be an example of this type of system. BT's AdvisorSpace system for its call center advisers, which I'll describe later in this chapter, would be an example of such a system.

As the degree of collaboration moves up into the integration model, applications that structure the process and the flow of the work begin to make sense. In a new product development environment, for example, lower-level engineers might have their work structured by a product life-cycle management system that keeps track of designs, components, and approvals for a major product design. Also within the integration cell would be systems for knowledge reuse—again, for example, in a new product development environment, where computer-aided design drawings might be reused. Reuse can also stretch into the collaboration environment, where an attorney, for example, might reuse a legal brief.

Decision automation, which I will describe in some detail later in this chapter, is suited for job roles with a middle level of structure and expertise, such as insurance underwriting. The lower-level jobs in such roles can be automated, but experts are still necessary to build and refine the system.

In the expert cell generally, the goal is to find some means of having a computer mediate the expert's work. If that's possible, then it is feasible to think about embedding knowledge into the flow of the work process, as I will describe in a health care application later in this chapter. Experts may also benefit from data mining and decision analysis applications for jobs involving quantitative data.

In the collaboration cell, as I argued in chapter 2, work is usually iterative and unstructured. The only types of tools that typically work in such environments are knowledge repositories and collaboration aids, which are used voluntarily. There could possibly be systems involving embedded knowledge, but these would be more difficult to develop and use in a highly collaborative work process. I will have more to say about many of these technologies later in the chapter.

Despite the power of technology to improve performance, not all forms of knowledge worker technology have been successful. There have been two pervasive dreams with regard to knowledge workers and technology. One is that knowledge workers would be able to easily access all of the data—typically data arising from business transactions—necessary to make decisions. The second dream is that knowledge itself—typically unstructured, textual knowledge—could be easily captured, shared, and applied to knowledge work. Neither of these dreams has been fully realized, but progress is being made toward their realization. It's taken much longer than anyone expected, however. What follows is a brief history of organizational technologies for knowledge workers.

Decision Support

In the late 1970s, a new idea emerged from academics who worked with applications of information technology. Called "decision support," the concept involved the use of complex computer algorithms to make data available for human decision making.[2] The dream of decision support proved to be a persistent one. IT academics in business schools found it almost irresistible, writing thousands of papers on the subject—perhaps many more papers than there were readers. Many vendors of software and services arose to sell decision support capabilities. The original concept evolved into Management Decision Support Systems (MDSS), Executive Support Systems (ESS), Online Analytical Processing (OLAP), Relational Online Analytical Processing (ROLAP), Multi-dimensional Online Analytical Processing (MOLAP), and so forth. Despite subtle variations, the basic concept remained the same, however: a computer program would churn through data and with human interpretation would reveal previously hidden trends and patterns that would allow an executive to make smarter and faster decisions.

However, the notion of computer-augmented decisions never really exploded like some other categories of computer software, such as ERP and database management. First of all, it was often difficult to extract decision rules or algorithms from human experts and put them in the computer—and the task didn't become much easier with the advent of artificial intelligence and knowledge engineering. Second, many knowledge workers didn't trust a computational black box to help them with decisions, preferring to rely on gut feel or other traditional approaches to decision making. A third issue is that it can be a time-consuming process to analyze the data needed to make a decision. The only decision support tool that did take off was a relatively primitive one—the Excel spreadsheet. Even with this simple tool, however, a high degree of human labor is often required to create and interpret the spreadsheets, and those created by inexpert managers and analysts are often rife with errors.

Artificial Intelligence and Expert Systems

Another idea that originated in the 1970s, and reached its fullest flowering in the 1980s, was the implementation of "artificial intelligence" and "expert systems." These technologies were supposed to eliminate or reduce the need for knowledge workers by extracting their knowledge and having a computer itself make important decisions or judgments.

This was an important idea, and as I'll describe later, organizations are still attempting to realize it. But at least in the first set of attempts, automating knowledge-based decision making didn't work out very well. A number of expert systems were developed, but pioneers in the field encountered numerous problems; for example:

- The knowledge intended for the system was difficult to extract from the expert's brain

- The knowledge in a system generally needed to change more rapidly than the system designers anticipated, and constantly revising for such change was difficult and expensive

- The best systems proved to be those that augmented human experts, rather than replacing them—which lowered the potential economic returns from expert systems

Knowledge Management

The first largely successful generation of organizational technology for knowledge work was known as "knowledge management."[3] This technology began to appear in the mid-1990s with the availability of Lotus Notes and later the Web, and became quite popular until the general retrenchment of information technology in the early 2000s. Knowledge management technology generally involved the creation of repositories—essentially databases—of knowledge. Organizations stored almost every imaginable variety of knowledge, including best practices, competitive intelligence, observations about customers, learnings from previous projects, and so forth. The most knowledge-intensive industries, including professional services, pharmaceuticals, and R&D functions within manufacturing, were all characterized by extensive development of knowledge management repositories.

But even this technology had its problems. It was expected that knowledge workers would find or contribute information in their spare time. The problem, of course, was that knowledge workers rarely had much spare time. As firms became increasingly lean and work processes became increasingly engineered, it became impractical to consult or contribute to knowledge repositories—particularly as some repositories became large and unwieldy. As economic conditions became more difficult and repositories became less valuable in the early years of the new century, knowledge management retreated in many firms.

However, repositories should not be entirely dismissed. There are circumstances in which they are probably the only feasible approach to supplying knowledge workers with the data they need to do their jobs. If a knowledge worker's job process is highly unstructured and collaborative, it is very difficult to determine in advance what knowledge and information a particular worker or position requires. And if there is no technological application that can mediate the worker's job, repositories may be the only alternative. This is the case, for example, with the collaborative jobs described in chapter 2. Jobs such as consulting or investment banking, for example, meet all the criteria described above. It's almost inconceivable that there would be an "investment banker's workstation" that would guide a banker through all the steps of the job, supplying information and knowledge as required. In any case, no one has yet built such a system, although such tools for similar jobs have been envisioned if not actually implemented.[4] Therefore, organizations in such industries will have to free up the time to enable their employees to seek and share knowledge from repositories.

Integrating Knowledge into the Job

What's the alternative to repositories as a knowledge management tool? One answer is to embed knowledge into the flow of the job process itself—the embedded knowledge applications that I mentioned above for expert knowledge workers. Under such an approach, knowledge workers don't have to seek out knowledge; it is delivered to them at the time of need. In fact, "integrating knowledge management into business processes" was selected as the most important issue of knowledge management in a 2002 survey of experts and practitioners.[5]

Are organizations flocking, then, to embed knowledge into the work processes of their knowledge workers? No, unfortunately— it's quite difficult to do this (I will describe some of the obstacles below). There are a few good examples, however. One of my favorites comes from Partners HealthCare, a group of Harvard-affiliated hospitals in Boston. Some other health care institutions are pursuing the same technology, but the Partners approach was both early and very well executed.[6]

While there are several ways to bake knowledge into knowledge work, the most promising approach is to embed it into the technology that knowledge workers use to do their jobs, which is what Partners has done for physicians. When knowledge supports the primary technology-enabled transactions used in day-to-day work, it is no longer a separate activity requiring slack time and the motivation to seek knowledge.

There are a variety of ways to bring knowledge to physicians in the course of their work, and Partners HealthCare employs several of them. Knowledge is embedded throughout the information systems used by its physicians. When a doctor prescribes a drug, orders a test, refers a patient to another physician, or even calls up the patient's medical record, logic modules and a knowledge base are invoked to potentially intervene in the care process. Referrals may be suggested by the system to be incorrect or unnecessary. Calling up a medical record may lead to a recommendation that certain follow-up tests or recommendations are desirable.

At the heart of its approach, however, is a computerized physician order entry system with trusted knowledge built in. The system may inform the physician that the patient is taking a drug that interacts with the drug being prescribed, or that the drug prescribed is not effective or economical for the indicated disease. In the case of test orders, it may note that the test is not generally useful in addressing the disease or symptoms identified, or that the test has already been performed on the patient sufficient times to indicate a diagnosis or treatment. A physician would use different systems (a referral system or a computerized medical record system) for some different transactions. However, all of these systems are integrated and all leverage a common database of patient clinical information and a common logic engine.

The order entry system is key to the delivery of quality medical care because ordering is where physicians execute their decisions about patient care; it is the point at which knowledge is most valuable. Without the system, there would be no easy way to apply knowledge at the time and place where it is needed most. Such an order entry system may increase both efficiency and safety, in the latter case by avoiding misinterpretation of poorly written orders. But the primary value is surely the ability to insert knowledge into the process.

There are, of course, times when physicians need medical knowledge when they are not face-to-face with a patient. For these circumstances, Partners has developed a patient "event detection" system that provides alerts to physicians via wireless pager when a hospitalized patient's monitored health indicators significantly depart from those expected. The physician can then proceed to directly observe the patient or call in a new treatment. The computerized medical record system can also generate reminders to physicians that a particular patient should receive a call, or schedule an appointment for a follow-up.

The power of knowledge-based order entry, referral, and computerized medical record and event detection systems is that they operate in real time. Knowledge is applied directly and immediately in the patient care process; the physician does not have to seek it out. In some situations, physicians can also get real-time access to experts for an online or telemedicine-based consultation.

Partners has also assembled many other sources of knowledge that are not real-time; this knowledge can be more extensive that that found in the logic modules, but it requires some time and the motivation to search it out. Online knowledge repositories (called the Partners Handbook) include online journals and databases, care protocols or guidelines for particular diseases, the interpretive digests prepared by Partners physicians, formularies of approved drugs and details on their use, and even online textbooks. All of these knowledge resources are accessible through an integrated intranet portal. While the resources available to Partners physicians are perhaps more extensive than those at other hospitals, similar resources have become widely available to those other practitioners as well.

Most Partners physicians also do research, so they may have a relatively high appetite for online knowledge. They are busy people, however, and their time to consult such resources is certainly limited. As a result the online Handbook is accessed, across all Partners institutions, about a thousand times a day. Contrast this with the thirteen thousand orders a day at one Partners hospital, Brigham and Women's, alone. The situation of these physicians is the same as that in which many businesspeople find themselves today: a wealth of online knowledge, but little time or context in which to peruse it unless it has immediate practical application.

While the Partners knowledge approach has been under development for over a decade, it's still not complete. The online order entry system and related knowledge are only accessible within the organization's two flagship hospitals, Massachusetts General and Brigham and

Women's. Medical knowledge has not yet been codified for all the diseases Partners physicians treat. The knowledge is embedded within several different information systems and is difficult to access. There is still plenty of work to be done.

Yet there is clear evidence that the approach is beneficial. A controlled study of the system's impact on medication errors found that serious errors were reduced by 55 percent. The ordering of a new drug that Partners experts found particularly beneficial for heart problems increased from 12 to 81 percent. When the system began recommending that a cancer drug be given fewer times per day, the percent of orders entered for the lower frequency changed from 6 to 75 percent. When the system began to remind physicians that patients prescribed a treatment of bed rest also needed a prescription of the blood thinner Heparin, the frequency of prescription increased from 24 to 54 percent.

These improvements save not only lives, but also costs. For example, recommendations from the system can point out drugs that are cheaper as well as more effective. Most significantly, a single adverse drug event (ADE) costs $2,000 in repeat tests, extra hospital days, and other costs. A typical seven-hundred-bed hospital will incur about $1 million per year in preventable ADE costs. To date, order entry with embedded knowledge is still rare enough that U.S. insurers have not yet seen their costs go down, nor have national malpractice costs declined. However, Partners, which insures itself for malpractice, has some early data suggesting that malpractice reserves can be smaller because there are fewer drug-related claims.

It isn't easy to develop such systems—either technically or managerially—and there are few off-the-shelf packages for knowledge-intensive business processes that would allow individuals and organizations to embed their own knowledge into systems. When Partners needed to create a complex information and technology infrastructure that would pull together the knowledge base and logic modules with an integrated patient record system, a clinical decision support system, event management system for alerts, an intranet portal, and several other system capabilities, it had to develop most of the systems itself. Other leading hospitals now have some or all of these capabilities, but Partners' real-time knowledge approaches are certainly at the leading edge.

However, the nontechnical and managerial aspects of the overall approach are just as important to its success, and perhaps harder to implement. Several of these issues—each of which would be relevant to any organization seeking to bake knowledge into work—are described below.

Motivation. How did Partners executives become motivated to develop the embedded knowledge approach? Embedding knowledge into work is time-consuming and expensive, so substantial motivation is necessary in order to undertake such an initiative. One key source of motivation at Partners was research that found surprisingly high levels of medical errors and preventable adverse drug events at Partners hospitals. That these leading institutions could be unconsciously acting in direct opposition to their healing mission was troubling, and it motivated action. The CEO of one hospital at which these errors were observed and measured, H. Richard Nesson of Brigham and Women's Hospital in Boston, insisted that there had to be a solution. The drug errors problem was the first that Partners took on, because much of the knowledge in this area is relatively straightforward and easy to program into an order entry system. As trust among physicians increased, Partners executives moved on to more difficult and complex domains such as patient care protocols.

Establishment of a credible and up-to-date knowledge base. When the knowledge of an organization is embedded into critical processes, it has to be of high quality and currency. If Partners employed idiosyncratic, obsolete, or untested knowledge in its medical care processes, it would subject its patients and itself to high risk. The organization has addressed this issue by forming several committees, and empowering existing committees, to identify, refine, and update the knowledge used in each domain. Medication recommendations in the system come from Drug Therapy Committees. Care protocols for particular diseases are designed by teams of specialists. Radiology Utilization Committees take on the task of developing logic to guide radiology test ordering. Leaders of clinical service lines (e.g., cardiology) are recruited to embed their particular knowledge into the system. Participation in these groups is viewed as prestigious, and busy physicians are willing to devote extra time to codifying the knowledge within their fields. Of late, Partners has been creating new umbrella organizations to oversee the knowledge bases across the organization, and to put the knowledge in a more accessible and manageable form.

Prioritizing which processes and knowledge domains to address. Since these embedded knowledge initiatives are difficult and expensive, they should only be undertaken for truly critical knowledge work processes. There are many different kinds of knowledge work jobs in hospitals and other knowledge-intensive organizations. Organizations should generally look first at knowledge worker roles that are critical to achieving the organization's mission and that may be bottlenecks for large bodies of important knowledge. At Partners, it was relatively easy to identify medical care processes as the most critical, but there were still important decisions to be made about which disease domains and which medical subprocesses to address (e.g., ordering medications versus referring a patient to a specialist) and in what order. Fields with many disease variations and multiple alternative treatment protocols (e.g., oncology) are more difficult to include in the knowledge systems. Partners executives are still trying to determine what types of knowledge resources would be most useful for other workers providing patient care (e.g., nurses).

Leaving the final decision up to the knowledge worker. With high-end knowledge workers such as physicians, it would be a mistake to remove the human experts from the decision-making process. They might either reject or resent the system if it challenged their role with patients. This was a mistake made by some organizations, such as those that implemented medical expert systems attempting to take over diagnosis, over the last couple of decades. Overreliance on computerized knowledge can also lead to mistakes. The approach taken by Partners is to present the physician with a recommendation. It is hoped that the physician will then combine his or her own knowledge with that of the system. On an average day at Brigham and Women's, out of 13,000 orders entered by physicians, 386 are changed as a result of a computer suggestion. When medication allergy or conflict warnings are generated, a third to a half of the orders are cancelled. The hospital's event-detection system generates more than 3,000 alerts per year; as a result of an alert, treatment was changed 72 percent of the time. These statistics are an indication that the hybrid human/computer knowledge system at Partners is working. Partners is now working on reducing the number of alerts to the minimum necessary, so that physicians won't feel the need to routinely override them for low-level concerns.

Developing a measurement and improvement culture. In order to justify both the effort and spending required for an embedded knowledge system, and to assess how well it's working, an organization embarking on this kind of initiative needs to have a measurement-oriented culture in place. Recall that the Partners effort was initially motivated by measurement of medical errors. The tracking mechanisms within the order entry system can detect whether physicians use the embedded knowledge and change their treatment decisions, which is the only way to know that the approach is working. Partners has always had a strong measurement culture because it is an academic medical center, and most senior clinicians are also researchers. But the development of this knowledge management approach has both enabled and required a greater emphasis on measurement of key processes. The measures are used as justifications and progress reporting tools for efforts to reengineer and continuously improve care processes.

Putting the right information and IT people in place. Whenever knowledge technologies are applied to business problems, it's tempting to attribute much of the benefit to the technology itself. But in the Partners case, and in many others I've seen, the improvement is heavily based on the employment of talented humans. Certainly it requires an IT organization that knows the business and can work closely with key executives and knowledge-rich professionals. A "back room" IT group could never successfully build a system of this type. For Partners, the management of measures, patient records, and knowledge also requires a staff that is skilled in information management. In health care this discipline is called "medical informatics," and Partners has recruited leaders in this field. It has several medical informatics departments, including Clinical and Quality Analysis, Medical Imaging, Telemedicine, and Clinical Information Systems R&D. The leaders of each of these departments are MDs, but they also have advanced degrees in such fields as computer science, statistics, and medical informatics.

Performance Support

The Partners case, and the general idea of baking knowledge into work, is new from the standpoint of knowledge management. However, it's not new at all from the perspective of organizational learning approaches. Well over a decade ago, for example, leading thinkers in the learning and training fields began to notice that training given substantially before a task was performed was not effective in improving performance of the task. Gloria Gery, in particular, wrote a book on this topic entitled *Electronic Performance Support Systems* in 1991.[7] It argued for just-in-time learning provided through electronic technologies—a vision that is remarkably similar to the just-in-time provision of knowledge I've just described at Partners.

Gery and her colleagues who advocated what has come to be known as "performance support" were correct, if ahead of their time. They were confident that the concept would penetrate industries during the next few years and change the way work and learning are performed in organizations. Unfortunately, however, all too few of these integrated work and learning environments have been actually implemented. Certainly there were some technological barriers to performance support, but even more problematic have been issues of economic justification, lack of understanding and sponsorship, and resistance from traditionally minded trainers. When performance support does flourish, however, it is likely to look very much like knowledge management that is embedded within work processes.

Role-specific Portals

The Partners example and performance support technology illustrate how powerful it can be to build customized IT applications with knowledge baked in. But there is another approach to delivering knowledge to knowledge workers that is halfway between a knowledge management repository and a customized application: the role-specific portal. A portal is a Web-based information delivery application that provides a range of information and knowledge on one site. A role-specific portal narrows that range by attempting to provide only the information and knowledge required for a particular role or job. Like a repository, it requires that the user search for the information, but it limits the scope so that the search is not difficult.

The information and knowledge accessible to the worker in a role-specific portal may be a mixture of transactional information, textual knowledge, multimedia educational content, and links to sites created by the user. The screen should provide all the information and knowledge necessary to do the job, and no more—otherwise the search would take too much time. Not all of the information on the portal need be unique, but views of commonly available information should be specific to the job. A great example of such a role-based approach is at the global telecom firm BT. The role on which BT has focused considerable effort is the "customer contact" worker or "advisor," of which the company employs fifteen thousand. While this is an example of a transaction knowledge work process, the focus for these workers was less on increased productivity (typically measured in call-handling times) and more on improved customer service through better availability of relevant information and knowledge. BT implemented a new role-specific portal, "BT AdvisorSpace," within its Customer Contact Centers. BT's goal is to make available all needed information and knowledge in real time while the customer is on the phone. One of the key design criteria for AdvisorSpace was to create an interface or 'portal' that focuses on delivering the information and functionality the advisor requires, as opposed to forcing the advisor to find the content via help files, intranet sites, and paper documents. Eventually the goal is to bring the relevant information to the screen automatically based on the context of the current customer transaction (i.e., to move more in the direction of the Partners order entry system).

The new system has already led to a several-percentage-point increase in the number of customers feeling that their advisor was helpful and knowledgeable (it's at 97 percent now). The advisors' confidence in the information they use is up by 23 percent. There have also been improvements in call-handling times. The BT example illustrates what an organization can accomplish when it focuses its efforts and information resources on a particular role.

As with Partners, BT focused its efforts on a single job. It's not possible to transform every knowledge work role at once. Organizations need either to select a role that is critical to its mission (physicians at

Partners, for example) or very numerous and expensive (call center representatives at BT).

Automating Decisions

The shortage of managerial time and analytical expertise that hindered the rise of decision support may be behind the rise of a new trend that holds the promise of realizing that dream, at least to a greater degree. With today's lean organizations, few knowledge workers have the time to delve deeply into data analysis or learn the intricacies of a decision support system (DSS). Instead of employing a DSS, many organizations are beginning to ask the system to make the decisions for them. Automated decision-making systems are penetrating a wide variety of industries and applications, and are taking over previously human-made decisions at least up to the middle management level. As I mentioned above, they also tend to be appropriate for middle levels of expertise and collaboration. With this approach, organizations can speed decision making, and lower the number of highly educated and expensive decision makers needed. This is not a new idea—it first took hold, for example, in "yield management" systems in airlines that made automated pricing decisions in the early 1980s—but the applications for the idea are expanding significantly. Sometimes called "in-line" or "embedded" decision support, the concept might be described as the intersection of decision support and artificial intelligence, or the "industrialization" of decision support.

After the success of yield management, automated decision making then became pervasive in the financial services industry and is still most common there. An increasing amount of information in financial services is available online, which makes it possible to integrate and analyze the information in more-or-less real time. In investment banking, these systems and online information are behind the rise of program trading of equities, currencies, and other financial assets. For most consumers, the primary impact of automated decision making is in the realm of credit approval. Credit scores, such as those from Fair Isaac Corporation (known as the FICO score), are used to extend or deny credit to individuals applying for mortgages, credit cards, issuance of telecommunications accounts, and other forms of debt. Although FICO-based credit scoring has been criticized for being overly simplistic, it has certainly made the process more efficient, and is behind the availability of near-instant credit decisions. Housing valuation information is also increasingly available online, making possible online mortgage and home equity loans in near-real time.

For example, Lending Tree, a marketplace of lenders for mortgage and other types of loans, uses automated decision-making technology to decide which lenders might be best suited to offer consumers a mortgage. Using seventeen different criteria, four banks are selected based on the likelihood they will close on a loan. Then the banks use either their own automated decision-making technology or software licensed from Lending Tree to make an immediate decision (within five minutes) on whether to offer a mortgage to the consumer and at what rate and terms to do so. Lending Tree guarantees that the consumer will receive all offers in one business day, but they typically come within minutes. Not only is the process much more efficient than that used by the typical mortgage broker, but Lending Tree has learned that the consumer is 10 percent more likely to accept a loan when it is offered immediately.

In financial services, automated decision making is being used for a broader variety of applications than just credit decisions. Citibank, for example, uses the technology for automated dispute resolution of credit card accounts. Mortgage banks have created automated systems to calculate nonstandard loan terms; a schoolteacher, for example, could get a loan that is only repaid during the school year. Most large insurance companies use the technology to underwrite most life insurance policies, and some are beginning to employ it for small-business insurance as well. Other firms have begun to use it to manage compliance to the mix of an investment portfolio. IBM Credit is using an automated system to assess the risk of its entire credit portfolio.

In consumer credit and collections decision making, several firms—most notably in the telecommunications industry—are beginning to use automated decision tools to move beyond binary decisions. Whether a person should be extended credit—or whether a customer with a past due bill should be denied further service—should not really be a yes-or-no decision. With more complex decision criteria, a cell phone company could decide, for example, that a customer with dubious credit is worthy of a pay-in-advance account, if not a regular credit account. Similarly, a customer who misses a single payment with an otherwise good credit history should be treated differently than a customer with a history of difficult collections.

Now automated decision making is penetrating into a wide variety of other industries. Some of the U.S. Middle Atlantic–area utilities that avoided the summer 2003 electrical blackout claim that they were able to avert the problem through automated decision making. An industrial equipment manufacturer is using the technology to determine the tax implications of various equipment contracts and to calculate services bills for maintenance. In insurance, automated decision systems are being used to process claims and underwrite insurance policies. In health care, they are being used to determine reimbursement levels.

In travel and transportation, where yield management once helped large U.S. airlines such as American fend off less technically sophisticated discount airlines such as People Express, automated pricing systems have become pervasive (no longer conferring advantage on the financially-hurting large carriers). The same tools are also now used in the pricing of hotels and rental cars. Automated pricing is also being employed for other types of products and services, including computers and electronics (at Dell Computer, for example), books (on Amazon), new car promotional offers (Ford), and even apartment rents.

Often these automated decisions are made within the context of a broader business process that is itself automated. "Decision engines" or "business rule engines" for automated decision making are increasingly being embedded within business process management (BPM) technology that orchestrates the entire workflow for a business process. Some observers call this process "smart BPM." If a bank, for example, were using the technology for credit card dispute resolution, it could not only manage the process from cardholder to bank to merchant and back again, but also embed automated decision making about how much and when to bill the customer.

Of course, these systems and processes can still involve some human review—either of all decisions, or a sampling of them. In many cases, particularly difficult cases are kicked out of the automated system to a human expert, and experts are also needed to help build automated decision systems and refine the rules they use. But the same constraints of time and expertise that limited decision support's rise will probably mean that few humans will be looking over the shoulders of automated decision systems. This will undoubtedly lead to considerable changes in how organizations view knowledge-intensive activities, and in the labor market for analysts and midlevel managers. Thus far automated decision making has been largely invisible to the public, but it may lead to a quiet revolution in organizations and societies. It also is not without risk: automating poor decision processes can quickly get a firm into trouble, and managers may not recognize the problem until there are substantial losses.

Other Types of Knowledge Worker Software

In addition to embedding knowledge in work processes, performance support, and automated decision making, there are a variety of IT applications that are intended to improve knowledge worker performance. These fall into a few specific categories, however, and are unlikely to be applicable to a broad range of knowledge worker performance issues.

One category is role-specific software for knowledge workers. These applications support a particular role that cuts across several different industries. Call center workers, for example, have at their disposal a broad range of technologies, though they are likely to have been chosen and implemented by others, not by the workers themselves. This is just one aspect of low-level, transaction-oriented work: there is little discretion about what tools to use in performing the job. Most call center agents, for example, don't have access to e-mail and the Internet from their office computers.

The applications for call centers include customer relationship management software, tools for scripting conversations with customers, knowledge tools for solving customer problems, and tools for capturing customer feedback. The goal of these applications is typically to increase the volume of calls that a call center agent can handle, and somewhat less often to increase the quality of service provided to the customer. Some organizations want to go even further and eliminate humans altogether from call centers, hence the rise of interactive voice response and other customer self-service technologies.

At the other extreme of role-specific technologies are tools for scientists in pharmaceutical, medical equipment, chemicals and petrochemicals, and environmental firms. Such tools as electronic lab notebooks (not necessarily notebook computers, but rather software for capturing the results of laboratory experiments) and laboratory information management systems have been available for many years, but these high-discretion workers have generally been given latitude as to whether and how the applications are used. If a scientist wanted to use a paper lab notebook, this was largely tolerated. The information and knowledge gathered were viewed as the scientist's personal property, so it didn't matter in what format it was gathered—at least if the scientist was generally productive.

More recently, however, companies have begun to insist that these tools be used in a consistent fashion. As laboratory documents become legal documents, and as laboratory information and knowledge becomes more critical to R&D and regulatory processes, firms are discovering that they can't leave the use of laboratory applications to the scientist's discretion. Infinity Pharmaceuticals, for example, a Cambridge, Massachusetts, drug development start-up that employs new approaches to chemistry and genetic screening, mandates that its scientists use electronic lab notebooks, and that they make their information available to everyone in the company. These tools, along with other scientific and analytical applications, have been combined into the "InfiNet Knowledge Platform," which is intended to provide a broad knowledge capture and knowledge sharing capability for the company and its research partners. As the importance of scientific productivity and knowledge sharing increases in this type of firm, we are likely to see more mandated use of the previously voluntary solutions.

Other technologies are more experimental, and not yet of clear value in the goal to increase knowledge worker performance. However, they offer the promise of enabling new knowledge worker functions and applications.

Social networking software, which I will describe in chapter 7, is one such category. This technology is intended to enhance the function of social networks both within and across organizations. Certainly these tools remind us that knowledge worker performance is not only an individual effort; ideas and their execution all derive from people working together. However, if it's difficult to measure and understand the performance of individual workers, it's even more difficult to determine how well social networks are performing overall. We're a long way from knowing how to assess the productivity of networks and the value that networking technologies bring to them.

There are other forms of "socialware"—software that supports social relationships—that some view as important to the future of knowledge work. Academics have studied this category for years, including technologies for finding people sharing common interests, for enabling a virtual conversation or discussion, or for group decision support and decision making. Most such activities have proven stubbornly resistant to any sort of automation, although occasionally a technology gets broader visibility and acceptance.

One example is Web logging or "blogging," which is a means for individuals to record their opinions for others to access. Partisans of blogging argue that there are many potential business applications of the technology (and they discuss these applications in their blogs!).[8] But I believe that blogging falls into the unproven category as far as knowledge worker performance is concerned. First, the business applications are largely hypothetical—at the moment it's a tool for individuals to express their somewhat random musings. Second, I know of no organization in which the benefits of blogging have ever been measured. Perhaps the biggest problem for blogging is the time it takes to write and read blogs. If anything this tool has detracted from productivity, not increased it. I am all for freedom of expression and self-publishing, but we shouldn't confuse the phenomenon with increased knowledge worker performance. One potential point in favor of blogging comes from my friend and former colleague Bill Ives, who argues that his own blog—and those of some others—is really a vehicle for managing his own personal knowledge. If this particular use of blogs caught on broadly, it could represent a new approach to organizational knowledge management.

Summary

Organizations need to strike a balance with new technologies for knowledge workers. They need to experiment and tinker with new technologies, and learn what their potential benefits might be for enhancing performance. But if they are to be used for business, a hard-nosed attitude should be adopted fairly quickly. What's the value? How should any improved performance be measured? Is the payoff equal to the cost—not just in hardware and software, but in the time required to learn, tinker with, and fix the technology? Ultimately, any evaluation of knowledge worker technologies will require close observation of how the technology fits into the context of the job. Learning and using new technologies is labor-intensive, and understanding their value and performance payoff is even more so.

All of the technologies discussed in this chapter have been at the organizational level, for organizational processes and objectives. But there is another world of technology and performance interventions that operate at the individual knowledge worker level, and this is the subject of chapter 6.

Recommendations for Getting Results from Knowledge Workers

- Information technology for improving knowledge work can be divided into two types: organizational and personal.

- Under the banner of "knowledge management," many organizations have created knowledge repositories to aid knowledge workers in jobs, but few workers have the time needed to browse and learn from repositories.

- An important alternative to repositories is the idea of embedding knowledge into the knowledge worker's job process. This is difficult to do, but can be very rewarding if done well—as in some health care processes.

- Performance support and role-specific portals are ways to reduce the amount of searching and browsing for time-pressed knowledge workers.

- Well-structured decision processes are increasingly being automated. In many cases, the work of entry-level knowledge workers is being done by computers, but experts are often still needed.

- There are many other categories of organizational applications for knowledge workers, including social networking software and blogging tools. These should be the subject of experimentation within organizations, but they have yet to demonstrate clear business value.

- Motivation to pursue knowledge technologies (such as the prevention of medical errors) is an extremely important factor in successful implementation.

6

Developing Individual Knowledge Worker Capabilities

Most interventions to improve performance in business are at the organizational or process level, but it doesn't have to be that way. We can also improve individual capabilities. Ultimately, knowledge worker performance comes down to the behaviors of individual knowledge workers. If we improve their individual abilities to create, acquire, process, and use knowledge, we are likely to improve the performance of the processes they work on and the organizations they work for.

Of course, some of the organization-level initiatives I've described also can improve individual performance, so what's the difference? Individual knowledge work improvement initiatives have two attributes. First, they are directly focused on improving performance of knowledge worker employees as individuals, not as members of a larger group. A CRM program for customer service workers doesn't qualify, because a number of people in that function would use it, and the system is not (or at least rarely) customized to individual needs. Second, individually oriented initiatives are targeted at improving some skill or capability, rather than instituting a new process. Giving knowledge workers a new piece of hardware or software—say, a personal digital assistant or cell phone—wouldn't qualify, but teaching them how to use these devices effectively would.

I became persuaded of the virtues of improving knowledge worker capabilities at the personal level when doing some work with the Software Engineering Institute at Carnegie-Mellon. The SEI is famous for its Capability Maturity Model, an assessment tool for software engineering processes that I described in chapter 3. It evaluates firms or business units on their overall approaches to software development. But Watts Humphrey, the developer of the CMM, had another key insight. He realized that it was taking too long for many organizations to move up through five stages of the CMM, and began to think about what might accelerate the process. He concluded that organizations would probably improve much faster if they were to develop team- and individual-level capabilities in addition to those at the organizational level.

SEI's research has borne out this hypothesis. Companies employing the *personal software process* (PSP) and the *team software process* (TSP) have been known to move from the lowest to highest levels of software development maturity in about a year—versus an average of close to ten years for this journey using only organization-level approaches.[1]

What Kinds of Capabilities Do Knowledge Workers Need?

The lessons of the PSP aren't, of course, relevant to all types of knowledge workers. Some individual capabilities are process-specific. In the

PSP, for example, software developers are taught and assessed on their ability to estimate, plan, measure, deal with data, and handle defects. Similarly, a consultant should focus on such capabilities as interviewing, presentation, and analytical skills.

But there are also generic knowledge worker skills that almost everyone employs, and that could benefit from improvement. What do all knowledge workers do? They read and write, of course, and our educational systems do a pretty decent job of inculcating these skills. Even that doesn't stop some assiduous knowledge workers from taking courses in speed reading, business writing, or the like. No doubt more of this should be done, but given the available resources for building this capability, there is no need to discuss it further in this book.

Knowledge workers also spend a lot of time in meetings. Most organizations, of course, don't do a very good job at helping their employees run meetings effectively. A few, like Xerox, have instituted organizationwide programs focused on maintaining a high quality of meetings. Again, there are plenty of written materials and educational options for people who want to learn more about meeting management, so I won't say anything more about it here.[2]

Increasingly, however, knowledge workers also process information and knowledge—on paper, in telephone conversations and voice messages, and electronically. This subject is much newer than reading, writing, and meeting, and there is relatively little information available about how to do it well, or how organizations can help their knowledge workers do it well. In this chapter I'll report on three research efforts to better understand this subject. Two were undertaken by a group of companies seeking to understand information work; both corporate and individual-level research projects were undertaken by this group. I'll also report on more detailed interviews of individuals who claim to be very effective in their own personal information and knowledge management.

Personal Information and Knowledge Management for Knowledge Workers

In 2003 the Information Work Productivity Council (IWPC), a consortium of technology and IT services vendors, funded a number of research projects on the topic of personal information and knowledge management (see "Research Approaches"). The companies and researchers participating in this project had realized that there was insufficient knowledge on how to get productivity out of information and knowledge workers, and all felt that this topic—personal information and knowledge management—would very soon become a major topic to be addressed by businesses. [3] One compelling reason for this was that information workers (people who use technology and work with information in the context of their jobs—perhaps a somewhat larger category than knowledge workers) were spending ever larger amounts of time (more than three hours per day by our data) messaging, creating documents, searching for information and knowledge, and other information-intensive activities.

Despite this large time commitment, information workers have been mostly left to their own devices, so to speak, with little help from their organizations in how to perform key information and knowledge tasks effectively and efficiently. And those devices, or the technologies used for handling personal information and knowledge, have been largely separate and unintegrated. Thus far our desktop PCs, laptops, wireline and cell phones, PDAs, handheld communicators, and other assorted technologies—not to mention the paper-based tools many individuals still employ—have been largely unconnected. At the same time that we face increasing technological challenges in managing personal information and knowledge, few individuals can be said to be well educated and well informed on how to use the tools to perform their jobs in an optimum fashion.

Research Approaches

THIS CHAPTER DRAWS from three studies of personal information and knowledge management. Two were performed under
the auspices of the Information Work Productivity Council (IWPC),
a consortium of technology firms founded to carry out research and
educational initiatives in the areas of understanding, measuring, and
enhancing information work productivity. In 2003, the year the IWPC
was founded, sponsoring firms included Accenture, Cisco Systems,
Hewlett-Packard, Intel, Microsoft, SAP, and Xerox. I was the academic director, and collaborated with several company representatives.
In the first of these studies, we interviewed twenty-one managers
in large companies and two government agencies who were interested in the issue. The particular managers we interviewed were typically knowledge managers, managers of new technologies, and IT
managers who dealt with personal productivity tools for their organizations.

The second study was focused on how individuals were dealing
with personal information and knowledge, and involved just over
500 U.S.-based information and technology users. These individuals
volunteered to complete a Web-based survey. We then reduced this
sample to 439 qualified respondents, all of whom had access to a
computer and e-mail at work, spent some time during the week processing work-related information, and used e-mail at least weekly.

The third study involved hour-long interviews with ten individuals
who reported that they were highly effective managers of their personal information and knowledge environments. They had a variety
of jobs across many industries.

Working with these devices to manage personal, work-related information and knowledge, however, is increasingly what people do within organizations. It's not hard to believe that with better technology, better education, and better management, the key tasks that information workers perform within organizations could be done with greater speed and quality, and at lower cost. Technology and information have become so closely integrated with work that better use of them can easily create more effective and efficient organizations.

Information Manager Findings

Information managers showed considerable variation in their orientation to personal information and knowledge management, with some companies already treating it as an important issue worthy of considerable attention, some on the road to that status, and some unaware—in roughly equal proportions. I suspect that the adoption of the idea will mirror that of other business and management innovations, and a focus on personal information and knowledge management will eventually spread and become much more pervasive. But there is much to learn from organizations that are addressing the issue today.

The leading-edge companies—found in the information and knowledge-intensive information technology, pharmaceutical, and financial services industries—exhibited a variety of traits suggesting that they were focused on personal information issues (see figure 6-1 for a graphic display of the orientations to these issues). Some were already actively dealing with personal information management with specific initiatives to address productivity through the use of technology. Cisco Systems, for example, had begun a "Change the Way We Work" initiative for employees, which involved a recommended set of technologies, education in how to use them, and a set of recommended behavior changes for optimum information-processing effectiveness.

FIGURE 6-1

Company orientations to personal information and knowledge management

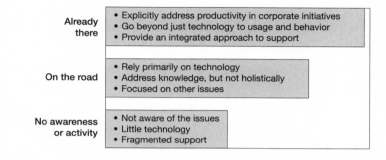

Capital One, the financial services firm, had a broad initiative under-way to improve individual-level productivity with technology (I mentioned their approach to experiments in chapter 3). Other companies in this category had similar programs under way, either for all employees or for a particular subset.

One of the earliest adopters of these approaches is Intel, which has created an "eWorkforce" initiative composed of three previous separate groups addressing knowledge management, collaboration, and personal productivity. The eWorkforce group has determined that better use of these technologies is a pressing problem for Intel, since its workers are aggressive users and spend large amounts of time doing so. Sixty-three percent of Intel employees participate in more than three teams; 62 percent routinely collaborate with people from different sites or regions; 40 percent regularly work with people who use different collaboration technologies and tools, and more than half work with people who use different work processes. Employees conduct 8,300 Web-based collaboration meetings and dial in to roughly 19,000 audio conferences every week. The group supports knowledge worker use of PCs, laptops, cell phones, and PDAs, and is developing integrated solutions for "generic" knowledge worker processes—tasks like arranging and conducting an asynchronous meeting or managing a project. Deliverables from the first phase of eWorkforce (just concluded as I write) included a consolidated collaboration platform, a standard project-management platform, next-generation meeting management, first-generation presence management (graphically indicating presence and availability) and instant messaging. In this phase, Intel also addressed the development of common processes and the use of best known methods for collaboration and group work.

These leading-edge organizations were making heavy use of emerging technologies such as instant messaging, PDAs, handheld communicators, and shared document repositories. However, their focus wasn't just on technology, but also on its use and the human issues behind the success or failure of technologies. These companies were generally making some attempt to change user behaviors and cultures—the Informatics and Knowledge Management organization within Novartis's research group, for example, had created a "Global Head of Knowledge Culture." Others were using technology itself to guide the changes in behavior. The support groups for individual users at these firms, like Intel's, were not specialists by type of technology, but had a holistic focus.

Other companies we interviewed were facing challenges with personal information and knowledge and were aware of them, but hadn't yet formulated a holistic response. I view them as being "on the road" to a focus on personal information and knowledge management. They were using some of the same emerging technologies as the leading-edge organizations, but the usage was less monitored and managed. There was a strong orientation to technology products as a means of dealing with personal information ("Our major project is changing from Lotus Notes to Microsoft Outlook"), but less focus on the use of those tools. There was generally no holistic support group for users of personal information, but in several cases a community was beginning to emerge across the relevant functions. In several cases, some major technology or business issue seemed to be preventing a focus on individual productivity, but discussion of productivity at a broader level was taking place within the company.

The companies in the third group were somewhat interested in the topic (or they presumably wouldn't have taken the time to participate in the interview process), but some were primarily focused on other issues—economic survival, for example. None of these organizations had really identified individual productivity as important enough to address with any seriousness, and generally did not recognize it as a corporate issue. They had no formal group to support even the basics of knowledge management or individual information use. What support they did provide to individual users was very fragmented by technology type. Little training or education was offered to users, and what was offered was product-specific. These organizations made little use of emerging technologies for personal information and knowledge or even discouraged their use; several specifically banned instant messaging, for example. Several stated apologetically that "we know we should be doing more in this area, but there is just too much else going on," or made similar remarks.

Measuring and Increasing Individual Performance

The early adopters' focus on individuals wasn't just a technology issue, but also involved an emphasis on productivity. Some necessary productivity tools and approaches, however, were lacking, although economic motivation was certainly present. Many organizations we surveyed—even the successful companies—were facing lower margins, reduced headcount to do the same work, and so forth. Most had some corporate orientation to increasing knowledge worker productivity, and technology and messaging tools were seen as vehicles to that end.

However, several firms complained that there were no good approaches to the measurement of productivity at the individual level. Several managers commented that the "time saved" approach to productivity (e.g., implement a new tool, and save thirteen minutes per day per knowledge worker) was no longer credible in their organizations. Productivity improvements at the individual level were viewed as yielding only incremental benefits, and for companies not on the leading edge, such investments couldn't compete with other categories of needed spending.

Several firms had a strong "self-service" approach to getting functional tasks accomplished, but a few respondents questioned whether that strategy was just shifting work to points where it is difficult to measure the impact. For example, if a company begins to ask its workers to perform all their own human resources transactions (choosing benefits providers, changing addresses, checking vacation balances, etc.), the cost reductions in the HR function can easily be measured, but how does it affect the worker's productivity? This problem needs to be studied in much greater detail to determine whether it's really helping organizational performance.

In order for firms to begin improving the management of personal information and knowledge, they also have to begin to change the behavior of users. There was considerable variation, even among the leading-edge organizations, about how this behavior change might best be created. As might be expected, for example, Microsoft's approach to behavior change is generally to try to elicit needed behaviors through the software it sells in the marketplace. All aspects of collaboration among knowledge workers, for example, should be handled by Microsoft's SharePoint collaboration software. If more human interventions are necessary, some Microsoft people would view this as a fault in the software. Intel's eWorkforce group, however, takes an approach centered on customized tools, process consulting, and job aids. Cisco is primarily focused on training as a means of creating behavior change. It is still too early to understand the implications of these differences and what might comprise a "best practice" in changing user behavior. The approaches of these leading-edge organizations have been driven thus far more by the culture of the company and the experience of the offering group, rather than by an empirical analysis of what really works.

There is also little consensus on how to segment information and knowledge workers for differential treatment. Most leading-edge firms, however, seem to recognize that they can't treat all their information workers alike, and are beginning to create segmentation approaches. I mentioned Intel's segmentation approach in chapter 2. At least three other organizations have an implicit or explicit segmentation by role— identifying particular roles and jobs that were numerous or important enough to justify an aggressive effort to design an information and knowledge environment around the role. Some other organizations, including information storage leader EMC and the engineering company MWH Global, are creating a taxonomy of roles within their organizations so that information and knowledge can be delivered on a role-specific basis with some precision. A third approach, employed by Xerox, among others, is the development or recognition of communities of practice, and the creation of information and knowledge environments that support those communities. As with behavior change, segmentation is in the early stages, and it's not yet clear which approach works best.

Overall, the information manager surveys confirmed that at least for some organizations, the problems and opportunities of personal information and knowledge management are real, and worthy of concerted management attention. Firms that make and sell technology, and those in industries in which effective personal information management and knowledge are critical to success, are believers in the idea and are already addressing it with initiatives. Other firms are either moving in that direction, or not doing anything at all. No matter how advanced on the issue, almost all companies are encountering issues of productivity measurement, behavior change, and user segmentation.

Information User Findings

Just as the information manager survey showed that companies vary widely in their approaches to personal information and knowledge management, our Web survey of information users also revealed a high degree of variance with regard to these issues. The intent of this survey was to discover the behaviors and attitudes of typical users of information technology at work, with particular emphasis on messaging and information distribution technologies. These activities are obviously of importance to individuals and firms, since, as already noted, the average person interviewed spent more than three hours on them each day—and it is likely that these numbers will only increase over time.

There is also no doubt that some people—about 20 percent on each of several questions in the survey—saw a substantial problem with their personal information and knowledge management. This fraction of individuals felt overwhelmed by their information flow, saw too much use of e-mail in their organizations, and viewed e-mail and other technologies as hindering rather than helping their productivity. On each of these issues the remaining 80 percent saw no real problem, although there were considerable differences in how much information they received and the media they used. Overall, few respondents would give up their messaging technologies, but some were frustrated with them.

It may be surprising to see just how much information and technology is used by the respondents of our survey. The average user in the survey:

- Spent 3 hours and 14 minutes a day using technologies to process work-related information—just over 40 percent of an 8-hour workday (see figure 6-2 for allocation)

- Devoted 1.58 hours/day to e-mail (45 percent of the information processing [IP] time, and 20 percent of an 8-hour day)

- Spent 47 minutes, or 24 percent of IP time, on telephone, conference calls, and voice mail

- Received 44 e-mails daily (4 people said they received around 500 a day!)

- Sent 17 e-mails daily

- Had more than 3 e-mail accounts

- Received 16 instant or text messages a day (for respondents using this technology)

- Received 18 calls, placed 15 calls, got 7.6 voice mail messages

- Participated in 2.75 conference calls a week (if any)

FIGURE 6-2

Average percentage of information processing time spent on each medium (based on average hours spent)

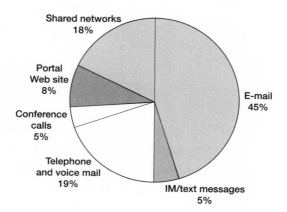

FIGURE 6-3

Percent of typical users (N=439) using each medium weekly*

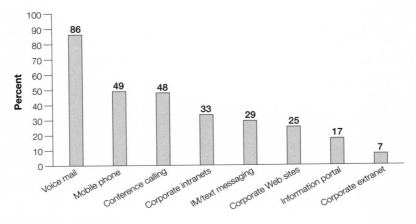

All use e-mail on a weekly basis.

The respondents' use of different messaging and information distribution technologies also varied widely. Figure 6-3 displays the frequency of use of the various media.

User attitudes toward their personal information flow and various media revealed further differences. 17 percent felt overwhelmed by their information management and flow, but this appeared to be more an issue of attitude than of volume of information. On closer examination, this group didn't receive more e-mails than average and didn't spend more time processing work-related information during the day. However, they felt they were less effective at managing information, felt that e-mail was less valuable to their work, and were substantially less likely to believe that they received help from their organization in managing information. Just under half of the sample, 49 percent, felt in control of their information management and flow.

Despite their complaints about personal information management, this sample illustrates Garrison Keillor's "Lake Wobegon effect"—that is, many believed they were better than average. Forty-one percent of our respondents felt that they were more effective at personal information management than others they knew; only 11 percent felt they were less effective. This finding speaks not only to the self-confidence of users, but also to the invisibility of how we manage our own information environments. We simply don't know how other people do it.

The overall lack of orientation of users to personal information management is suggested by an open-ended question in our survey. We asked respondents what one thing they would change in their personal information environments, and then categorized the responses. The most common responses were "nothing," with 16 percent, and "don't know," with 13 percent. Among more substantive responses, 11 percent would reduce spam or pop-up ads, and 7.5 percent would limit the amount of e-mail. Other answers were too idiosyncratic to report. The large number of uninformed responses suggests that most individuals have not thought very much about this issue thus far—and that they have probably underinvested in their own personal information environments—which other researchers have suggested.[4]

The survey also asked respondents to what degree their organizations helped them manage their personal information flow. Forty-one percent said that they received little or no help from their organizations in managing personal information; only 3 percent felt that their organization had completely mastered the problem of personal information management. This confirmed my expectation that most organizations have a long way to go before they have fully dealt with this set of issues. However, individuals may feel that they are doing all they can, and since they aren't getting much help from their organizations, in the absence of any direction or contrary evidence, they may feel they are doing fine.

Attitudes Toward Specific Media and Technologies

E-mail was one of the most frequently used media in the study, and also one of the most problematic in terms of negative attitudes. In our sample, 26 percent felt that e-mail was overused by their organizations; 10 percent felt it was underused, and 64 percent believed it was being properly used. At the individual level, 21 percent felt overwhelmed by the amount of e-mail received and sent, 41 percent felt that e-mail was very or extremely valuable to their work performance, and only 4 percent felt it was not valuable. Although 15 percent felt that e-mail diminished their work productivity, 53 percent felt that it increased it. On balance, the responses of the users were positive about e-mail, but less positive than for some other messaging and information distribution technologies. For the roughly 20 percent reporting a significant problem with e-mail, the key question is whether they are ineffective at managing it, or they are just more conscious of its negative effects than others.

Survey questions involving the telephone—actual telephone calls, voice mail, and conference calls—elicited somewhat fewer negative attitudes than about e-mail, and somewhat more positive attitudes. Only 12 percent (versus 21 percent for e-mail) felt overwhelmed by the amount of telephone calls and messages they received. Almost half, or 49 percent, felt telephone information to be very or extremely valuable to their work performance—8 percent more than for e-mail. Respondents assessed the impact of telephone calls and messages on their productivity similarly to that of e-mail, with 15 percent concerned that the telephone diminished their productivity, and 50 percent believing it enhanced their productivity. About the same percentage (14 percent) felt that voice mail diminished their productivity; 40 percent (10 percent less than telephone calls) felt it enhanced productivity. Only 4 percent were overwhelmed by the number of conference calls they participated in, but a relatively low percentage (35 percent) felt that conference calls were very or extremely valuable to their work.

Instant messaging (IM) was apparently still an emerging medium for this sample, with lower overall perceived value. Among our respondents, 56 percent didn't yet have IM use in their organizations. Among those who used the technology, 29 percent felt that IMs and text messages were very or extremely valuable to their work performance—substantially less than for e-mail or telephone-based technologies. A slightly higher percentage than for other technologies (18 percent of those who use IM) felt that it diminished their productivity; 35 percent felt it enhanced productivity—again, lower than for other technologies.

Perhaps the most popular technologies were those involving information and knowledge "pull" rather than "push." These are corporate Web sites, information portals, and document sharing systems. Those who used these tools reported low levels of being overwhelmed (4 percent) and diminished productivity (4 percent), with high levels finding these technologies very or extremely valuable (47 percent for corporate Web sites, and 64 percent for document sharing systems) and productivity enhancement (4 percent report diminished productivity, 50 percent enhanced for Web sites; 3 percent diminished, 67 percent enhanced for document sharing systems). The positive reaction to document sharing was the highest for any technology in the study. As the amount of information in organizations continues to proliferate, these technologies are likely to become even more popular.

Strategies for Managing Information

The survey also included questions on how these information users were coping with the types and amounts of information they received. The majority of respondents reported using specific approaches to limit or control their personal information. These varied by technology. For example, the strategies respondents employed for dealing with e-mail are illustrated in figure 6-4.

FIGURE 6-4

Percent of typical users (N=439) employing e-mail management strategies

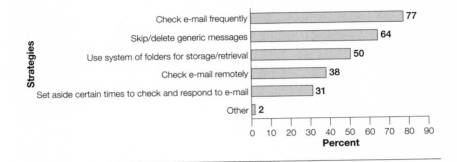

FIGURE 6-5

Percent of those using IM/text messaging weekly (N=131) employing IM management strategies

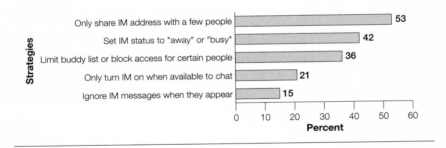

Similarly, figure 6-5 shows the strategies respondents regularly employed to manage instant messaging.

The most popular strategies for managing voice mail messages were:

- 61 percent responded to voice mails immediately.

- 59 percent checked voice mail frequently.

- 40 percent skipped uninteresting messages in the first few seconds.

The most popular strategies for managing information on portals or corporate Web sites were:

- 58 percent reviewed information on the site on a regular basis.

- 55 percent bookmarked key pages and added shortcuts.

- 46 percent used browser functionality to find what they needed.

The most popular strategies for managing document sharing and shared networks information were:

- 57 percent reviewed and updated files on a regular basis.

- 54 percent bookmarked key pages and saved folders as favorites.

- 38 percent checked sites/files when they received notifications or alerts.

Clearly large numbers of users were not reacting passively to information overload, but were taking active steps to reduce the amount of information they received, organize their information, and integrate information processing activities into their daily work environments. These were not particularly sophisticated coping mechanisms involving advanced technologies or highly evolved information preferences, but they do suggest that people aren't just letting information roll over them.

Differences Among Groups

There were a few interesting differences across demographic groups in the study.[5] In some cases, differences may be explained by other factors (e.g., differences between older and younger workers may be explained by different jobs that they typically hold).

There were a few differences between men and women in our sample with regard to information processing and technology use.

Women, for example, processed information for 26 minutes a day more than men. However, men were more likely to be "information foragers," being 9 percent more likely to have mobile access to e-mail. Men were also 7 percent more likely to believe that software tools helped them to avoid information overload (we men have always loved tools!).

One might expect to find that younger people would be more likely to communicate via technology and to be on top of their personal information environments. It didn't turn out that way. For example, people age 45 to 54 received at least ten more e-mails per day than other age groups. Use of instant messaging—again often thought of as a technology for younger people—increased with age to the 35-to-44 category, and then fell off sharply in the 45-to-64 group. People 35 and over were 14 percent more likely to feel in control of their information management and flow, again contradicting our expectations.

There was, however, some confirmation of common stereotypes. Those under 35 were 7 percent more likely to have mobile access to e-mail, for example. People under 35 were 13 percent more likely to say that they are effective at information management than those 35 and older, so the young were relatively confident. Respondents under 35 were also more likely to rely on software tools to filter out e-mails they didn't need to see, and to let dealing with e-mail expand into their personal time. The 35-and-older group was less technologically oriented but more discriminating, being much more likely to delete and ignore unimportant information, and to apply strict guidelines about what information received attention.

Respondents represented three levels within their organizations: senior executives, middle managers, and individual contributors. The business stereotype would suggest that senior executives would rely primarily on face-to-face communications, while more junior workers would communicate electronically. To my surprise, senior executives were the heaviest users of electronic messaging technologies. For example, senior executives received more than twice as many e-mails as middle managers or individual contributors/professionals, and sent significantly more as well (overall this analysis is not quite statistically significant across all groups, but is for senior executives versus everyone else). Even more surprisingly, senior executives and middle managers sent and received more than twice as many IMs as professionals/ individual contributors. Middle managers and senior executives were also 11 percent and 7 percent, respectively, more likely to have mobile access to e-mail than individual contributors. Senior managers were 20 percent more likely than middle managers to feel that they were in control of their information flow, and 7 percent less likely to feel overwhelmed by it. It would appear that the heavy use and control of information by senior executives is not because they receive high levels of assistance from their organizations. Senior executives were 7 percent more likely than middle managers, and 5 percent more likely than individual contributors, to feel that their organizations provided little or no help with information management. They felt that they needed more help, but weren't getting it.

Finally, respondents were asked whether they were in general/ corporate management, an MIS or IT function, or some other type of department. There were several significant differences across these groups. General/corporate management and corporate MIS/IT people used e-mail more frequently than other departments, and sent and received more e-mail. Ironically, corporate MIS/IT people were not fully convinced of the value of their offerings; they were 20 percent more likely than senior or corporate management to believe that e-mail is overused. However, MIS/IT people were 12 percent more likely than senior managers, and 10 percent more likely than other departments, to believe that instant messaging is properly used (and also more likely to feel that voice mail is properly used). But like senior executives, general managers were 22 percent more likely than MIS people, and 15 percent more likely than other departments' employees, to feel in control of their information flow.

One final group we analyzed was based not on demographics, but on usage. "Heavy users" of communications technologies were defined as those who used at least four different media for communications, each at least weekly. I suspected that this group might be bellwethers for the future. Just over a third, or 34 percent, of the survey respondents fell into this category. Not surprisingly, the group used information heavily in the course of their work. These users were 21 percent less likely to spend two hours or less processing information, and more likely to spend between two and a half and eight hours processing information. But they were not necessarily positive in their feelings about at least one technology. The heavy users were 13 percent more likely to feel that e-mail is overused, and 7 percent less likely to feel it is underused. They were somewhat polarized in their attitudes toward e-mail and their own productivity; they were 9 percent more likely to feel that e-mail diminished their productivity, 5 percent more likely to feel it enhanced their productivity, and 14 percent less likely to feel it did not affect their productivity at all. In short, those who made heavy use of technology seemed a bit concerned about its value to their own work and their organizations. This suggests a growing problem that will probably become more pronounced over time.

Individuals Who Have Mastered the Problem

To address the question of mastery, I worked with another researcher, Dave Clarke at the American Red Cross, to interview ten individuals who claim that they are highly effective in managing their own personal information environments. This may not seem like a large number, but I believe the incidence of people in this category is very low. I often ask audiences to whom I speak to raise their hands if they are highly effective at personal information management. Less than 1 percent—even among corporate information and knowledge managers—identify themselves in this category.

Of course, as I've noted above, we don't know much about how others manage their personal information streams, so people could be better than they think. Although the ten individuals interviewed were fairly modest about their own information management proficiency, they uniformly said that others came to them for help in finding obscure information or for insights about how to use technology to manage information. The ten individuals held a variety of jobs: they included a fundraiser for a private school, the administrator for the board of directors of an automobile company, a venture capitalist, a consultant/researcher in a large firm, an independent consultant, a technology manager for a nonprofit organization, a director of member services for a nonprofit research organization, a knowledge manager, an editor, and a professor.

These highly proficient personal information managers weren't all alike, but they had some things in common. Several of their common attributes are described below:

- *They avoided gadgets.* One—the technology manager—tended to try new tools (including a BlackBerry and a notebook computer) because it was part of his job, but dropped them quickly if they didn't prove effective. The rest, however, found a few key tools—hardware and software—and stuck with them over time. A couple were Palm Pilot devotees. One did virtually everything within Lotus Notes. There were several heavy Outlook users. But they were universally conservative in adopting new tools. Most of the tools were well-known, although the venture capitalist was a strong advocate of a piece of software called "the Brain," and a couple were experimenting with new tools for searching personal files.

- *They limited the number of separate devices.* One did everything on his laptop, and had abandoned several home desktop computers. Another was very enthusiastic about his Treo cell phone/PDA combination—in part because it reduced two devices to one.

- *They invested effort in organizing information.* One came into the office every Sunday for a couple of hours to prioritize his "to do" lists and organize his information. The venture capitalist had to participate in a large number of conference calls, and he used them to organize his files and folders.

- *They weren't missionaries.* While people came to them for help, they provided it, but most didn't feel sufficiently capable to broadly advertise their skills. There was one exception to this principle, however: an individual who constantly proselytized about the virtues of better information management within his office. Even he admitted that some people found this tiresome, and his supervisor felt even more strongly, telling us in a brief conversation that the person's activities were "a waste of time." Shortly afterward, he left the organization.

- *They got help.* They didn't attend a lot of courses, but they read manuals and called on support people for help. Several had gotten instruction by searching the Internet. One individual asked a database manager to explain to him the structure of the key databases in the organization, so that he could access information more easily.

- *They used assistants—to some degree.* Most of the people I interviewed have some degree of administrative support available to them—what used to be called a secretary. These individuals relied on their assistants to schedule and confirm meetings, make travel arrangements, and handle some communications. Yet the informationally proficient seem reluctant to turn everything over to their assistants. None of this group, for example, relied on an assistant to read and answer e-mails, though a few utilized their assistants to help with some voice mails. Perhaps e-mail was too personal to entrust to someone else, or my respondents' ability to type (universal, I think, in this group) made them inclined to handle anything involving that task. Or perhaps the general decline in the level of administrative support in many organizations made it infeasible to turn everything over to an assistant. In any case, the role of assistants would seem to be crucial in effective information management, but it seems to be declining in my small sample.

- *They weren't doctrinaire about paper versus electronic approaches.* Though several of the people said they were trying to reduce the role of paper in their informational lives, nobody was fully electronic. Several said they still used paper calendars, or printed and carried around paper copies of electronic calendars.

- *They decided what information was most important to them, and organized it particularly well.* The professor had online folders for every article or book he'd written, and had a special program for capturing and organizing citations. The venture capitalist had an Excel spreadsheet that summarized the financial situations of all the companies he was involved with. The board administrator had Notes files for every issue that came before the board.

- *They use lists.* Most weren't slavish about it, but there was general agreement that lists can be freeing, as David Allen has suggested in a series of books and conferences.[6] These individuals kept lists of appointments, things to do, contacts, books to read, and so forth. Some used electronic lists, some used paper, and one individual wrote particularly important things to do on the back of his hand. "Since I got my Palm Pilot, however," he commented, "I rarely get all the way up my arm now."

- *They adapt the use of tools and approaches to the work situation at a given time.* The researcher in a consulting firm, for example, had always believed that instant messaging was a waste of her time and attention. Her primary job was to conduct research and create research reports, and even though IM was becoming a culturally important aspect of her firm, she resisted its use. However, she moved to Prague for a six-month period, and during that time was working on a project with several consultants that required close collaboration and less solitary concentration. She adopted IM and used it extremely heavily during that period. She felt it was extremely useful not only in doing the collaborative task, but also for reminding people that she was around and available, even though geographically distant. Whenever she felt that something was important in an IM message, or a request was being made that she couldn't respond to immediately, she would copy the contents of the message and send it in an e-mail to herself. Now she is back from Prague and off of that project, so she uses IM more sparingly, and turns it off whenever she has a report to write or a research issue to think through. She also neglects e-mail during these periods, even though her unavailability violates some unstated cultural norms in her firm.

Consistent with the data from the corporate and individual surveys I reported on earlier in this chapter, most of these people didn't get a lot of help from their organizations. None of their companies or organizations had made personal information management a general priority. None had any holistic interventions available to make people more effective at managing personal information and knowledge. Though there are coaches available to help with this sort of thing, none of the participants in this little survey had ever availed themselves of such coaching. For the most part, they figured it out on their own. [7]

Summary

I believe that the field of personal information and knowledge management is poised to take off. Companies and individual employees are beginning to focus on it, new technologies are increasingly being introduced to address it, and the business case for improving personal productivity is becoming increasingly clear.

But this is clearly a field in transition, with considerable variation in awareness and behavior. Some companies and individuals are seriously wrestling with the issue and taking action on it. Several have specific initiatives to improve the ways their employees manage their information and knowledge. And a good proportion of individuals are concerned about the effect of technology and information on their personal productivity, and are taking active steps to manage personal information so they don't become overwhelmed.

A second group sees the problem, but isn't taking concerted action. It's probably only a matter of time before they overcome their inertia and begin to respond. At the corporate or organizational level, this would mean going beyond a focus on technology products for personal information management, and addressing how people use them. It would also mean uniting previously fragmented approaches to supporting individual-level technology and information users. At the individual level, it would mean investing personal time and energy in improving one's own information environment, and seeking help both inside and outside your organization.

A third group of organizations and individuals clearly don't get it yet. These companies and government agencies, and their individual users, don't have personal information and knowledge management on their radar screens, so they're not likely to do anything about the problem anytime soon. These less-aware organizations may be composed of a lot of individuals who don't care about the issue, and hence don't put any pressure on their companies. Perhaps when consultants and vendors and authors begin to address the issue, these organizations and individual users will start moving on it.

Of course, personal approaches to improving information and knowledge management are only one solution to the problem of knowledge worker performance, just as this is only one chapter in the book. The only way we can truly go astray with the technologies and methods of personal information and knowledge management is to adopt them without attending to the other factors that can improve knowledge worker performance that are described elsewhere in this book. One of them is social networking, which I describe in the chapter 7.

Recommendations for Getting Results from Knowledge Workers

- Most interventions to improve knowledge work performance have been at the organizational or process level, but sometimes improving the capabilities of individual knowledge workers can dramatically accelerate improvement at the organizational level.

- Perhaps the single most important, yet rarely addressed, knowledge worker capability is the management of the personal information and knowledge environment.

- Some companies have begun to address the personal information and knowledge environment, going beyond the simple provision of tools and technologies. They take a holistic approach, address productivity at the individual level, and offer interventions such as coaching or education to make knowledge workers more effective.

- Most knowledge workers have personal strategies for dealing with all of their electronic information, but they aren't very sophisticated; there is much room for improvement.

- The few individuals who are confident that they have mastered their personal information and knowledge environments have much more sophisticated strategies, including minimizing the number of devices they use, learning one piece of organizational software very well, and devoting considerable time to organizing and managing their information flows.

7

Investing in Knowledge Workers' Networks and Learning

What's more important to improving knowledge worker performance: technological networks or human networks? Consider the following observations from a strategy consulting manager interviewed for the research I describe in this chapter:

> I think what distinguishes me is an ability to solve problems and move things forward quickly and in a generally correct direction . . . and a lot of this does come down to my network. I am not calculating about my network or someone that hands out cards at conferences, but I do make it a priority to take care of it. And this pays off over and over. When I need information or help on something people return my calls because they know I will be there for them. And I can't tell you the number of times that a relationship or doing something for someone pays

off later on. It might be two or more years, but taking care of good people in my network almost always seems to come back to benefit me in big ways.

Technical and social approaches to improving knowledge creation and sharing complement each other, but they emanate from preconceived notions of how knowledge workers get information and solve problems at work. While knowledge worker performance is critical, we know little about how high performers within that category get information and knowledge from other people, learn from their experience, and solve problems in their work. In 2003 I undertook a study with Rob Cross of the University of Virginia and Sue Cantrell of Accenture to determine how high-performing knowledge workers leverage their informational environments.[1]

We studied the social networks of knowledge workers in four organizations that received high performance reviews. Second, we conducted interviews with high performers in each organization to learn how they maintain expertise and develop/employ their personal networks.[2] In this study my colleagues and I were trying to reveal the work habits and strategies of the people we want to emulate—the high performers in knowledge-intensive work (see "Research Approach").

Our approach is similar in some respects to that of Robert Kelley, who carefully observed high-performing knowledge workers at Bell Laboratories.[3] Kelley focused on the individual attributes of knowledge workers, such as their willingness to take initiative. He did note that "networking" is an attribute of high performers, but didn't investigate this area deeply; thus far we know little about the attributes of those social networks. In this research we attempted to find out how high-performing knowledge workers get information and solve problems at work, with a particular focus on social networks. By developing insights into how such workers acquire information and knowledge, and use them to solve problems, we can then better design holistic management solutions—from appropriate leadership behaviors to organizational design and HR practices—to support this work.

How Knowledge Workers Find and Use Information

How do high-performing knowledge workers get information and solve novel and complex problems at work? In part, of course, they solve difficult problems by relying on their own knowledge and expertise. A substantial challenge for all knowledge workers is maintaining and extending their expertise. However, in today's knowledge-intensive environment, it is rare for any one person to know enough to solve increasingly complex and interdependent problems. For example, consider today's medical profession, where physicians must coordinate knowledge from their own minds, online resources, specialists, and even their patients, who may have more time to review massive amounts of information related to their specific problem. It's been estimated that a general practitioner, for example, needs to know about a million facts—clearly difficult without external help of some sort. These and many other categories of knowledge workers must be effective at finding and assimilating external information and knowledge as necessary.

One way knowledge workers do this is by relying on impersonal sources of information such as databases, the Internet, publications, or formal courses. These are treated in other chapters of this book. A second, and often overlooked, way that people get information to solve problems at work is through their social networks. Consider your own experience for a moment. When you last faced a new challenge such as starting a new assignment or important project, did you get the critical information you needed by typing in search terms on the Internet or by seeking information from colleagues or friends of colleagues? Most people choose the latter. In fact, research over the past twenty-five

Research Approach

WE SET OUT TO understand how high-performing knowledge workers found information and learned how to do their work via a mixed method research approach in four organizations. Each of the groups we studied consisted of middle managers or professionals and were targeted because their work was knowledge intensive but different in character. The first two groups we worked with—72 electronics technicians supporting oil drilling in a major petrochemical organization and 102 specialists providing advanced sales and maintenance support for a major electronics organization—worked on "things." Their work was highly knowledge intensive yet focused on physical objects. In these settings, there are right answers and feedback—performance of a drilling rig or a nonresponsive electronic component provides very real guidance as to what solutions are effective. The output of the second two groups—112 strategy consultants from a well-known consulting firm and 68 information scientists in a leading technology organization—was ideas. There are many "right" answers in the world of the second group; these knowledge workers are less constrained by rules or physical reality and so may seek out information very differently. Being able to assess all four groups allowed us to generalize lessons both across different organizations and unique kinds of knowledge work.

years consistently reveals that people rely heavily on other people to find information and to learn how to do their work.[4]

Individual Expertise

Interestingly, we found little correlation between traditional measures of expertise (e.g., education, tenure, and self-rated expertise) and high performance. To be sure, lack of expertise predicted poor performance (i.e., bottom 20 percent), but expertise alone did not consis-

In each organization we obtained annual performance ratings for people we surveyed. A major criterion for choosing the companies we worked with was that their performance management systems were reliable and overall ratings were based on both objective and subjective assessments from several vantage points.[a] We conducted surveys to understand correlates of performance on several fronts. First, we were interested in levels of expertise as reflected in education, tenure, and self-report information. Then we collected two kinds of network information in our surveys: (1) personal networks that could entail important contacts from both inside and outside the organization and (2) bounded networks where people characterized their relationships with coworkers *in their groups* (e.g., the strategy consultants or the technicians) to assess how they were connected to their colleagues. We then conducted semistructured interviews with 40 of the high performers; each interview lasted approximately an hour.

a. This ensured that the view we had of performance was both reliable and mattered in each organization for important decisions such as promotion and compensation. In profiling high performers we took the 80/20 rule to heart (i.e., 80 percent of the work is done by 20 percent of the people). Specifically, we looked to see what distinguished the top 20 percent of performers across the organizations. While there were some unique findings in each of the organizations, what we present here are the consistent points across organizations.

tently distinguish high performers. Rather, as I'll describe below, it seemed that high performers were more intentional, flexible, and proactive learners over time.

Internal Networks

We used social network analysis to assess the relationships among each group in terms of both information flow (i.e., seeking information from others) and awareness (i.e., "I am aware of this person's expertise").

While the first network provides a snapshot of information flow in a group based on a current portfolio of projects, the second view represents a group's ability to tap into expertise of others when new opportunities or problems come along. In terms of information flow, high performers were heavily sought out for information, having on average six more people routinely coming to them for information than average performers. And the reverse is true for low performers. They were much less likely to be sought out and, unfortunately, much more likely to be taking the time of a high performer.

High performers tended to have a paradoxical pattern to their networks. On the one hand they tended to have stronger relationships with a few colleagues, who themselves were well connected within the network. These relationships were rated highly and also reciprocated, and seemed to provide a basis of support or help for getting work done. On the other hand, the high performers also nurtured diversity in their networks and were more likely to have bridging ties into other pockets of the network. Specifically, they were more likely to have ties into physically distant locations of the organization, reaching up in the hierarchy and to those with more tenure (and presumably expertise) than low or average performers. Perhaps these relationships provided them with unique information, and helped them to capitalize on opportunities.

In terms of awareness of others' expertise, we found what we expected. High performers were aware of the expertise of more people in the network and more likely to be aware of people in subgroups or pockets in the network. This of course is an important asset to the high performers, in that they can rapidly reach out to others when new opportunities or problems come along. The reverse was also true—many others in the network were aware of these high performers' skills and expertise. This is potentially important in a different light, in that reputation itself can be an important asset to an individual.

Personal Networks

We also used a social network approach that allowed respondents to identify those they considered most important to them from an informational perspective. In this phase of the survey our respondents listed people both within and outside of their groups and organizations, so that we could assess external relationships critical to high performers. Here we again found some important differences between high performers and the rest of the pack. First, high performers were likely to maintain and leverage more relationships than average performers. And in particular, high performers tended to have more ties reaching both outside of their departments and outside of their organizations.

In addition, high performers tended to have more new people in their networks (i.e., people they have known for less than five years). This type of pattern would seem to promote more effective learning, as one does not get locked into a specific set of advisers that might not be relevant to the tasks at hand. Tapping into those with the most expertise (as opposed to those with whom we are comfortable) is sure to help improve work and problem solving in these settings. Finally, high performers invested more time in developing and maintaining these relationships than did the rest of the knowledge workers. Thus while the high performers might not be overly social or political about networking, they do seem to be intentional about maintaining the relationships around them.

Overall, our survey results provided us with some interesting insight. Principally we learned that while maintaining a level of expertise and utilizing technical resources improved performance (i.e., at least kept people out of the bottom 20 percent), these did not seem to be the key distinguishers for high performers. Instead, high performers were distinguished by larger and more diversified networks that allowed them to both become aware of and rapidly take action on new projects or opportunities. Of course it is a stretch to say that there is one right network structure for everyone; task demands, individual expertise, organizational factors, and many other issues come into play in dictating an effective network pattern. However, it's clear that diversity along some of the lines just mentioned is helpful.

A Ground-Level View of High-Performing Knowledge Workers

To gain more insight into these high performers, we conducted interviews with forty of them across four organizations. Our intent was to get a rich view of the strategies high performers employ in finding information and solving important problems at work. We emerged with a set of consistent practices used by high-performing knowledge workers. First, they engage in certain activities that keep them on the cutting edge of their own expertise and help them develop new capabilities as appropriate. Second, they are proactive and intentional in developing, maintaining, and leveraging relationships around them. As a result, high performers are able to tap into others for information more effectively, and other people bring opportunities to them more frequently. Finally, they are adept at maintaining a "good enough" information environment that enables them to fluidly juggle information and priorities.

Effective and Efficient Experiential Learners

We couldn't tell from our interviews and analyses that high-performing knowledge workers had more formal education than lower performers, or that they were smarter to begin with. Rather, our interviews suggested high-performing knowledge workers were effective and efficient experiential learners. They tended to make good decisions in investing time and effort in developing new domains of expertise.

These domains often were not natural extensions of current expertise as defined by a given career path, but helped these high performers to integrate diverse expertise and skills.

High performers also seemed to get more learning out of a given experience and continually updated their skills, expertise, and social awareness as a natural part of their work. This continual learning allowed them to benefit from each experience, whereas others might compartmentalize learning to classes, or fail to leverage work as a vehicle for learning and improvement. One new project manager explained, "I learned management not from a class, but through reflecting on my past experiences of being managed, through simple trial and error, and through conscious observation and reflection on the acts of other managers."

Many high-performers attributed problem-solving abilities to the acquisition of a broad base of knowledge. Knowing how one's work impacts another department or function, seeing opportunities to collaborate or help solve a problem in another part of the organization, or understanding how two seemingly different kinds of expertise fit together were typical traits of high performers. Explains one manager, "My success relative to my colleagues is due to the fact that I can marry the financials with a thorough understanding of the business. My colleagues, on the other hand, are focused on only one perspective or the other."

Our high performers often had unusual, and often somewhat illogical, career paths. However, they repeatedly told us in various ways that these different jobs provided them with unique perspectives and expertise in solving problems. In general, we found that lateral moves, unrelated projects, or work that built expertise or perspective within an organization allowed high performers to "see" opportunities that more parochial colleagues might miss. These projects also built a diverse network that could be leveraged as needed—again, an asset that more insular colleagues did not enjoy.

Of course, not following a predefined career path within an occupation or organization can be a risky strategy. Seeking out new experiences, knowledge, and expertise can also be risky if these experiences do not help to distinguish an individual. Explains one electronics technician who decided to take on a new role as an expert in Deming's quality control methods, "I had always been moving up in the organization—operations was the path to the top. Taking on this new role was incredibly risky. It could have easily become just another program that was sidelined (and me along with it)."

Although the high performers in our study took risks, they characterized themselves as "calculated" risk takers who considered the pros and cons of investing time and effort into a new domain of expertise. Rather than simply jump to an opportunity too early or with little thought, they considered projects, rotational assignments, or their expertise development efforts as means to distinguish themselves in the future. For example, one software developer commented:

> When I came here there was a huge pressure to jump on some Web-based applications. Everyone was pushing in this direction and it was, in many ways where the investments were being made. I kept thinking that it might not be a good long term bet in terms of skills and expertise and so focused on different areas. In hindsight this has been a key way that I have distinguished myself. Even if the dot-com bubble hadn't burst, I think it allowed me to develop some more unique capabilities rather than going along with the herd.

But when they do make a decision to pursue a given area of expertise, the high performers invest heavily, and seem to have a "compass" for personal learning. They often described themselves as highly focused on the domains they decided to pursue. Their focus often required fending off other demands on their time or calls for them to become knowledgeable in other areas. However, it also allowed them to excel in the areas they had chosen and to develop a reputation for expertise that drew other opportunities to them. As outlined by one consultant:

> You get a thousand calls in this place. People want you to have something bright to say on pretty much anything at all times. I think this can get you distracted and actually hurt you. I think the thing that has been best for me is to say "OK, I will try to keep up on certain issues, but I am going to really stay on top of this one and develop expertise here so that others are coming to me." It sounds easy, but there are a lot of distractions that can take you off course.

High performers not only reach out to master new domains; they work hard to maintain the knowledge in domains they might already have mastered. Rapidly evolving technologies and new management approaches demand that knowledge workers constantly refresh and update their stores of knowledge. High performers tend to use very different strategies for learning new domains, however, than they do for maintaining knowledge in existing domains. Most high performers turn to specific, known sources of information to maintain their knowledge. Although they rely to some degree on certain Web sites, industry publications, e-learning tools, books, and other externally published information, they rely most on their contacts in personal networks.

People were described as being the most efficient source of learning, because of their ability to screen out irrelevant information, provide alerts to new and important information in the field, and condense or expand information to the appropriate level of detail required. Often, knowledge workers will quickly browse codified sources of information and then turn to people to "fill in the holes." Explained one knowledge worker, "I can ask people specific questions and therefore not waste time. With a class, only 10 to15 percent of the content is ever relevant to my specific needs." Added another, "Learning through courses or written material is too much of a time sink. And with people, you can get behind the PR to get the real story."

Investing in Personal Networks

Personal networks are critical resources for learning and solving problems at work. Our high performers provided vivid examples of how their networks allowed them to capitalize rapidly on new opportunities or solve tough problems at work. High performers were able to leverage others quickly for their expertise when specific information was needed. They also often checked ideas and perspectives with others to ensure that they were thinking about issues in a sound way. One software executive related:

> Especially early on in a project when things are fuzzy I am
> bouncing ideas off of the best people I can get to. This might
> mean technical people to see if the concept is feasible and effi-
> cient, or marketing people to see if it will fly. Really, though, I
> am just trying to nail down the important areas to focus on and
> this has a lot to do with the later success of the effort. Without
> a good network I would not be able to get the input at such a
> critical stage.

Although a popular conception of assiduous networkers is that they are highly political and career-focused, we rarely heard high performers talk about using their networks toward political or career advancement ends. In part, it seems that our high performers rarely have to. By spending their time getting work done rather than posturing or pursuing political agendas, these people developed reputations and networks that brought them opportunities and resources; they talked about networking much more as a human process of connecting well with others and looking for points of mutual benefit over time. Unlike "social butterflies" building numerous surface relationships, our high performers focused on quality relationships helpful for them in the present and the future. Three tactics seemed instrumental in this pursuit:

Establish a personal connection. Almost all important relationships in our high performers' networks were characterized as more than just business contacts. All relationships that had become important assets on a business front had also developed along a personal front as well. For example, people might discover similar backgrounds, family experiences, or hobbies that allowed them to connect on more than just an instrumental basis. These personal connections made contacts more helpful and more willing to commit time and effort to a high performer's cause. They also improved the quality of problem solving; when personal connections existed, our high performers were more willing to take risks with ill-formed ideas and to be more creative in brainstorming. These core contacts in our high performers' networks were also critical for expanding their networks, as new contacts were usually made through referrals from people in their core networks. Only a few high performers relied on "cold" contacts for information, and usually only as a last resort. One engineer we interviewed explained:

> For years, I didn't consciously maintain my network. That's a mistake. If you want to be successful, you have to develop and cultivate relationships. They need to know and trust that you are someone they can talk honestly to. Relationships don't work without trust; I go out of my way to cultivate it and maintain my relationships. I spend a lot of time making phone calls and sending periodic hellos through e-mail to check in with people and keep my network alive.

Follow through. High performers put a high priority on accomplishing tasks and responding to people in a timely manner. A surprising number of people operated on an unwritten "thirty-six-hour rule" of responding to e-mails and phone calls, and nearly all spoke of the importance of "acting on and keeping commitments." Doing what you say you will do not only gets your work done, but also allows people to rely on you to come through. It also builds trust critical for knowledge transfer. One consultant indicated the importance of this:

> People have to know they can count on you if you're going to be in their heads when opportunities come up. Probably all of us have been burned by people who talk a good game or make commitments and never come through. This can have big implications for your career if you are taking risks in front of a client or with your boss . . . the important relationships in my network are ones I know I can rely on and vice versa, we treat each other with importance and this creates a scenario where everyone is better off in the end.

Proactively reciprocate. High-performing knowledge workers don't just demand information from others, but also actively offer information and opportunities to those in their networks. Many described their networks as "two-way streets"; the only way they will receive information is if they make a point to give information in return. But giving and receiving knowledge seems to be done in a noncalculated, natural way. One information scientist explained, "If I get something interesting by e-mail, I make a huge point of disseminating it to others who might be interested. I try to share knowledge as much as I can. But I don't think of it as a 'favor bank' of knowledge in which knowledge is exchanged tit for tat." Sometimes high performers even go out of their way to make sure the person receiving the information can readily absorb and understand it. One information scientist we spoke to, for example, makes a point of tailoring the format of the information when she can to the person receiving the information.

Juggling Information and Priorities

If the use of technology to manage information doesn't distinguish high performers, what does then? Without prompting, one high performing information scientists told us, "The single biggest factor contributing to my success compared to others is the ability to juggle and prioritize all the information that is constantly coming toward me. I never let people hang on too long, and I always get things done. But I don't juggle by using technology; it is more of a mental balancing act and way of being than anything else." Adds another high performer, "The thing that sets me apart from others is that I constantly keep on top of, and reshuffle, what I need to do. As information comes to me, I keep it organized (in my head, through keeping my pending e-mail list short, and on a paper 'to do list') so that I am sure to act proactively, not reactively." And finally, "I am most successful because I get it done and get it done on time. I can pull it together when it's not obvious how to pull it together."

High performers also have an ability to "surf" and allow for the emergence of a problem, project, or opportunity. These people have picked up on one of the fundamental shifts in today's knowledge-intensive work that challenges managers and executives at all levels—both problems and solutions are much more emergent than planned. This makes it difficult if not impossible to design environments and technologies for organizational or personal productivity. Emerging problem areas suggest the right resources (both people and informational) to bring to bear, and remaining flexible until the problem has become better-defined allows the high performers to get to better answers.

Managerial Implications

There are several implications for managers interested in better supporting high performers and their practices in organizations. I will highlight a few below, but perhaps the most important point to consider is the interrelated nature of these practices of high performers. Their approaches to experiential learning, technology use, and networks are highly intertwined, building on and reinforcing each other. For example, being strong experiential learners helps high performers win a reputation for both having expertise in an area and being a good colleague. This reputation certainly helps to support a rich personal network, and is a source of opportunities as others seek out the high performer when they need help. In addition, our high performers' breadth of expertise and varied backgrounds provided them with unique insights and perspectives in doing their own work and sensing opportunities. These perspectives are enacted through diverse networks and are supported by fluid information environments that allow them to see, fit together, and convince others that a given opportunity is emerging.

Networks

While network development might be somewhat innate to a given person, we also found that managers can do a lot to support effective network development in their organizations. Perhaps the most important point here is not to equate networking with socializing or more communication. Very rarely do overburdened knowledge workers want more offsites or meetings for purely social objectives. Rather, helping employees develop an awareness of who knows what in the organization allows them to know whom to turn to for help. Job titles and organization charts alone provide little guidance as to whom people should seek out when a new problem or opportunity comes along. In part this can be facilitated by such technologies as skill profiling systems or expertise locators. However, technical solutions have to be wed to interventions that promote the quality of relationships and collaboration in these settings. Forming communities of practice, for example, is a largely relational approach that pairs well with expertise location systems.

The entire human resources chain can affect collaboration by informing the kinds of people brought into the organization, the way in which they are developed over time, and the behaviors that are measured and rewarded. A distinguishing feature of organizations with more cohesive networks is often that the managers recruit for collaborative behaviors. For example, they might employ a "critical incident technique" (asking a potential employee to identify incidents in which he or she solved a tough problem, for example) to seek evidence of collaborative behaviors. Alternatively, some organizations require recruits to demonstrate collaborative behavior in the hiring process via a group problem-solving exercise. In the words of one manager in the strategy consulting firm: "The problem solving in these things is horrific, but you get a very, very accurate view of who is going to work well in a collaborative environment." Of course the key is to make sure that hiring decisions are influenced to some degree by what is learned—it does no good to interview for these behaviors but then base the final hiring decision only on individual accomplishment or personal chemistry.

Once workers are in the door, career development practices can also have a significant effect in helping these employees nurture and sustain effective personal networks. They can assist employees both to assess the current composition of their networks and to develop plans to improve connectivity in targeted ways. Though largely absent in the organizations we studied, personal network development was emphasized significantly by the strategy consultancy in our group. This organization took professional development plans seriously and incorporated some component of network development into them. Anecdotal results suggested the approach was working, as employees recounted scenarios of winning work or delivering high-quality client solutions based on ways that their networks enabled them to pull together expertise for a client.

Performance evaluation is also an important HR process that can promote collaboration at critical points in networks. For example, some organizations use performance appraisals that assess an employee's collaborative behavior on a given project. Others have designed annual evaluations requiring people to demonstrate that they have supported cross-division efforts. Still others use 360-degree evaluation processes that ask people from other units of an organization if they have been supported by a given person. Formal rewards in organizations clearly signal whether collaboration or individual achievement is important. The point is to understand the extent to which collaborative behaviors are truly valued above and beyond lip service. It is obviously counterproductive to advocate the need for collaboration and sharing, and then show employees what really matters with reward systems that encourage noncollaborative colleagues.

Beyond HR practices, leadership and culture can have a profound influence on networks. Some leaders in our study were quickly described as just naturally capable of promoting rich, dense networks. Rather than trying to consolidate their own authority, these leaders shared information and decision making, connected people around them, and drew peripheral people into the network. The leaders most effective at network building tended to envision tasks as challenges demanding collaboration with others, either within or outside their department. Rather than break tasks apart in an effort to pinpoint individual accountability, these people fostered robust patterns of collaboration in the well-functioning social networks we assessed. This belief in the importance of collaboration was also signified by problem-solving sessions where opinions were actively solicited regardless of hierarchy or experience.

These leaders were also unique in that they sought out and celebrated effective collaboration rather than just heroic individual effort. The leaders were described as being quick to acknowledge collaborative work in public forums, offer spot rewards to those who went out of their way for others, and promote people who were collaborators. In both word and action these leaders sent unambiguous signals on the importance of collaboration. And leaders of better-connected networks tended to be more aware of interpersonal tensions within the network that could have a detrimental effect on collaboration and coordination. This did not mean that they themselves were highly skilled at interpersonal interventions; quite often they brought in facilitators to avoid taking sides on an issue. Regardless, they did have the awareness and courage to deal early with tough interpersonal issues (either between themselves and others, or among members in their group) rather than ignore the issues and let them fester.

Finally, an important role of leadership is to communicate, model, and reward behaviors supportive of a collaborative culture. Specific cultural values also exist in organizations that can preclude effective collaboration. For example, the oft-cited "not invented here" (NIH) syndrome is, in many cases, rooted in a history of successful invention and self-reliance that has evolved unchecked. Low-trust environments often keep employees from reaching out or sharing ideas early in the problem-solving process. Yet this is precisely where others' knowledge and expertise can be most beneficial—before problems become rigidly defined and a course of action dictated. In these settings, leaders have an opportunity to articulate the kind of collaborative behaviors they are looking for and then to model and reinforce them on a daily basis.

Experiential Learning

Knowledge workers can also benefit from training on experiential learning techniques. If most knowledge workers learn new things mostly through experience, how can we help them consciously adopt strategies to improve this learning? One strategy that is well known, but still often overlooked, is to institutionalize the "after action review" throughout an organization to ensure that some learning takes place after an event.[5] This technique is simply a structured approach to reviewing the learning from an initiative immediately after it is concluded. Some interviewees also mentioned mentoring programs as being particularly useful; again, knowledge workers appear to learn best from each other.

Allowing learning from failure is another cultural attribute that can contribute to experiential learning. Humans fail, but organizations often don't let people acknowledge failure, or learn from it. Senior executives can set a powerful example by admitting their own failures and describing what they have learned from them.

A third approach to encouraging experiential learning is to hire for it. If the best performers are those who learn from experience, then recruiting processes should focus on identifying individuals who appear to have taken on experiences in order to learn from them, and who can articulate what they have learned to others.

Technology

Information technology can be used for knowledge-related activities other than searching for text in an online knowledge repository. Companies are beginning to explore technologies that facilitate the development and use of social networks. While many social networking tools are primarily targeted at individuals, some focus on developing contacts within organizations. For example, many companies have developed expertise directory or "yellow pages" applications to point knowledge seekers to those who have it. Hewlett-Packard was one of the first firms to develop such an application.[6] Their system, Connex, was originally intended to identify experts within HP Labs, but has since been used for a variety of other units within the organization.

More recently, organizations have begun to use social networking software internally. For example, 3i, a leading global venture capital and private equity firm, uses a "relationship intelligence" system called InterAction to help achieve its "one-room company" corporate strategy while expanding its global presence. With more than six hundred investment professionals operating in sixteen countries, 3i needed an application that would enable colleagues within the organization to communicate with each other and also provide visibility into the firm's collective network of strategic relationships, both inside and outside the company.

For instance, in a recent buyout deal, 3i wanted to approach a German company to buy one of its French subsidiaries. The U.K. team members leading the acquisition did not personally have the high-level relationship needed, so they turned to the software to determine if another 3i employee might. Utilizing "Who Knows Whom," one of the features built into InterAction, they uncovered a colleague working out of the Milan office who had a relationship with the target company's mergers and acquisitions director. This colleague agreed to secure the needed introduction, and the deal was subsequently awarded to 3i. The firm expects to garner profits in the $25-to-$50 million dollar range from the buyout. "I found it compelling that someone on the U.K. team was looking for an opportunity, the business was in Germany, and the strategic relationship we found was in Italy," said 3i's head of HR. "Without InterAction, it would have been unlikely that we would have uncovered this strategic connection."[7]

Granted, this description is taken from InterAction's marketing communications materials, and things may not flow so smoothly outside of that idealized realm. But companies should not ignore the possibility that software and computer networks can facilitate social networks. Just think what our networks would be like without e-mail!

Summary

My colleagues and I undertook this research to understand better how high performers get information and solve problems at work. By focusing on the best knowledge workers in our sample organizations we sought to surface tools and practices helpful to aspiring high performers in various settings. There were some fairly consistent points of differentiation, particularly in the network realm, between high and average performers. We expected to find some differences in how knowledge workers at "idea-based" firms manage information and solve problems, compared with knowledge workers at "product-based" firms. Yet we found fairly minimal differences, which further supports the importance of these overall practices of high performers.

Most importantly, perhaps this work will help correct some misperceptions between the practices of knowledge workers and how some might think they get their work done. Far and away, the predominant interventions in knowledge management have focused on technology. While I don't question the importance of technology in organizations today, it's only one source of knowledge and learning for knowledge workers. We invest more in e-learning tools than in mentoring programs, for example, but most workers do the majority of their learning through experience and people rather than through e-learning. These results suggest a need to redirect some of the investment knowledge-based organizations make to practices that nurture social networks and human capital.

Recommendations for Getting Results from Knowledge Workers

- Technological interventions into knowledge work can be useful, but high-performing knowledge workers say that they get most of their valuable information from other people in their social networks.

- High performers are more likely to be sought out for information than are lower performers, and also have stronger and more diverse networks to which they can turn for information. Helping all knowledge workers improve their networks could create more high performers.

- High performers also have more ties reaching outside of their organizations, making them effective boundary spanners. They also have more ties to new employees, making them effective at transmitting knowledge and culture during the "onboarding" process. Both these areas could be further cultivated.

- High performers learn not only through people, but through a diverse set of work experiences that they insert themselves into. They take calculated risks in their jobs in order to secure new learning experiences. This type of learner should be sought in recruiting processes.

- High performers actively manage their networks, but not primarily for political or self-advancement purposes. They know they receive a lot of information through network contacts, so they are careful to reciprocate with information and nourish network relationships. If more employees adopted these behaviors, they'd have better networks too.

- High performers use technology, but they also juggle a lot of information in their heads, and employ paper as well. Problems and solutions for them are more emergent than well-defined. Technologies offered to knowledge workers should reflect these preferences.

- There are a variety of ways that managers can facilitate the growth and effective functioning of social networks. Software is emerging for this purpose, but is largely unproven— except for e-mail.

8

The Physical Work Environment and Knowledge Worker Performance

One factor that affects knowledge worker performance that isn't well understood is the physical work environment—the offices, cubicles, buildings, and mobile workplaces in which knowledge workers do their jobs. There is a good deal said about this topic, but not much known about it. Even more unfortunately, most decisions about the knowledge work environment are made without seriously considering their implications for performance.

In 2002 I and my then-colleagues at Accenture Bob Thomas and Sue Cantrell undertook a study of this issue.[1] We interviewed forty-one companies that had some initiative under way intended to improve the performance of high-end knowledge workers, or those with particularly high levels of expertise and experience, who were critical to the organization's mission. We were interested in all the factors that affected knowledge work performance, but the topic most commonly addressed by the companies was the physical work environment (the other common ones were information technology and management, and I've also devoted at least a chapter to each in this book).

The introduction of a new workspace was most often the catalyst for a broad redesign of the knowledge work environment in our study. Because it is so tangible, a new or alternative office can be both the symbol and a key part of the reality of new ways of working. For example, Pharmacia recently built a new pharmaceutical research building outside of Chicago that was intentionally designed to encourage more interaction among its R&D staff. The new workspace was intended not only to attract top research scientists to the company, but also to promote a more collaborative culture. Particular designs can encourage certain types of behavior, although they will never guarantee it. Of course, office space is also expensive, and savings resulting from decreased or alternative space often serves as a rationale for change.

Workspace design is a somewhat faddish phenomenon, in part because no one knows exactly what factors affect knowledge worker performance, and how those factors interrelate. In the absence of knowledge, vendors of office environments, architects, and developers are free to make all kinds of claims about what works. But we do know some things from the limited amount of research on this topic, and in the next section I'll provide a list of what is generally agreed to be true with regard to the physical work environment. Then I'll describe a framework that will help managers think about the physical environments for knowledge work in their own organizations.

What We Know About the Physical Work Environment

From either previous research, logic, or common sense, there are a few things we know about the relationship between physical work environments and knowledge worker performance. They include:

Knowledge workers prefer closed offices, but seem to communicate bet-ter in open ones. Of course there is great variation among open and closed office types, but the most extensive research in the area (from Cornell professors Frank Becker and William Sims) suggests that while most knowledge workers prefer closed offices because they are better able to concentrate, they communicate informally and build trust and social capital more easily in more open office environments (even high-walled cubicles, they say, restrict interpersonal communi-cations). They note: "Our research, done with employees in job func-tions ranging from software development to marketing and business development, indicates that the more open the 'open' plan office en-vironment, the more conducive it is to overall work effectiveness, when communication and interaction are critical elements of the work process."[2] Becker and Sims are undeniably experts on this topic, but I feel that, like many corporate executives, they downplay the need for concentration and quiet when knowledge work is done in office environments.

Knowledge workers congregate in particular geographical areas. This factor has been made well-known by Carnegie-Mellon professor Richard Florida in his book *The Rise of the Creative Class.* He docu-ments the fact that knowledge workers (not synonymous with the "cre-ative class," but closely overlapping it) are drawn to, and are made more productive by living in, cities and regions with concentrations of other people like themselves. Silicon Valley, Boston, and Austin are prominent examples of this phenomenon, at least for knowledge workers oriented to information technology. The connotation is that if you're a knowledge worker or a business that needs to hire them, you need to find out where the center of action in your industry is, and lo-cate yourself there. If you're a city manager or mayor and you want these successful, taxpaying individuals to live in your city, you need to make your city attractive to them and to the businesses that hire them.[3]

Knowledge workers move around in the course of their work. They need mobility and spend a lot of time out of their offices. Several firms that have observed their knowledge workers have found that they spend up to half of their time out of their offices—either in meetings, talking informally in other peoples' offices, or traveling. As a result, organizations need to provide them with the ability to work and be productive outside of their offices. The most obvious instantiation of mobile work environments is the laptop computer, but there are others—for example, access to physical work artifacts such as books and files, the ability to use telephones, computers, and messaging technologies while traveling.

Knowledge workers collaborate. They meet, they chat, they congregate. Office environments need to facilitate the collaboration and exchange of tacit (hard to express in explicit written terms) knowledge. What does this mean? At a minimum, there need to be meeting spaces and conference rooms. Maximum facilitation would be to create a variety of collaborative spaces, technologies, and facilitation approaches for an array of collaborative purposes. Technologies for collaboration—from videoconferences to webcasting to shared networks—are increasingly making a big difference in collaboration, but users are frustrated by technical difficulties in many cases.[4] Very few, if any, organizations have attempted to foster collaboration to a high degree, in part because they haven't made the effort to understand what kinds of collaboration are needed.

Knowledge workers concentrate. The opposite side of the collaboration coin is the need to concentrate at work. This requires a quiet setting with relatively few distractions. Such an environment is particularly important for knowledge creation activities—thinking, writing, programming, designing, and so forth. This takes up a widely varying proportion of knowledge workers' time—some studies have found, for example, that programmers spend only 20 to 30 percent of their time doing solo programming, but others have found workers devoting up to 64 percent in "quiet work."[5] Whatever the fraction of time, it's important for the production of final knowledge work outputs. Many organizations that have moved to more open offices trumpet the benefits of increased collaboration, but they discount the penalties incurred on the concentration side.

Knowledge workers work in the office. Despite many years of discussion about telecommuting and telework, a very small percentage— some studies suggest 5 percent—of workers do "serious" (full-time or near-full-time) telecommuting, and a good proportion of those are administrative workers rather than knowledge workers. Knowledge workers, like all other types of workers, like flexibility, and they like to work at home occasionally. However, they don't want their homes to be their only offices. They know that to be constantly out of the office is to be "out of the loop"—unable to share gossip, exchange tacit knowledge, or build social capital.[6] This means that organizations should not bother with office arrangements that assume full-time telecommuting, even though occasional telecommuting doesn't save companies any money. It also means that firms that are committed to telecommuting may be less attractive in the knowledge worker labor market.

Knowledge workers communicate with people who are close by. Tom Allen, the dean of researchers on the work behaviors of scientists and engineers, found more than two decades ago that technical workers (a proxy for knowledge workers) whose desks are more than thirty meters apart have a frequency of communications that is roughly zero.[7] Some might argue that e-mail and instant messaging have changed the relationship between physical proximity and communication. However, I'd argue that you rarely e-mail or IM intensely with someone you don't know. Assuming it's still true, Allen's important and oft-cited finding means that companies should design work environments so that knowledge workers who need to communicate are physically close to each other. Of course, this requires some strategizing about who needs to be talking with whom. Organizations such as 3M and Herman Miller have tried to do just that in the design of some of their facilities.

Knowledge workers don't care about facilities gewgaws. At least there is no evidence that anyone ever took a job, stayed at a job, or worked more productively because of foosball, pool, or ping-pong tables, cappuccino bars, office concierges, hearths, conversation pits, quiet rooms, lactation rooms, creativity rooms, relaxation rooms, nap rooms, etc., etc. In these lean and mean times, many workers are even reluctant to be seen using these facilities for fear that they won't be considered hardworking enough. In any case, there's no clear relationship between knowledge worker performance and various appealing features of the work environment, though they may help slightly with recruiting or morale. To my knowledge only a couple of office furniture firms (Herman Miller and Steelcase, to be precise) do much to have an impact on such workplace innovations—and their focus is on broad workplace changes, not on architectural gewgaws—so we may never know for certain whether they are worth the money and the architect's time.[8]

Despite the faddish nature of workspace design and the absence of detailed knowledge on its implications, many organizations truly believe in the effects of the particular approaches they have adopted. It is often assumed, for example, that open offices lead to increased collaboration and open communication. This was the goal at SEI Investments, where all dividers were torn down in favor of a big open room that, according to one SEI knowledge worker we interviewed, "creates a fun environment in which people can communicate freely." Of course, an HR manager at SEI admitted that only about half of the potential hires for the company thought they could stand working in such an open environment, which seems a high price to pay for architecture (although, to be fair, SEI believes that the environment is a good screening mechanism for the collaborative workers they want to hire).

Certainly there are many occasions in which chatting over cubicle walls has facilitated the flow of information through knowledge work processes. Yet we heard just as many anecdotes about workers who stayed at home to do heads-down work because they couldn't concentrate in the office. One knowledge worker involved with highly sensitive political risk analysis, for example, feared that his job performance would be severely compromised as soon as the firm moved to a completely open floor plan. And at Monsanto (which later merged with Pharmacia & Upjohn to form Pharmacia), where a business unit had attempted to do away completely with private offices to reduce hierarchy and increase communication, senior officers of the unit eventually erected their own private offices. Employees are skeptical of open office arrangements and often suspect (as do I) that the primary benefit of these designs is the lower space costs of packing more people into cubicle-structured space.

Similarly, mobility within the workspace and outside of it is a frequently cited objective. This obviously makes sense in industries such as professional services, where workers must travel to clients frequently. Yet we don't know what price organizations pay in social capital when employees are highly mobile and can't be easily located for a face-to-face conversation. "Hoteling," for example, or the assignment of workers to whatever workspace is available when they come into the office, is clearly an efficient means of allocating space to mobile workers, but several firms that have experimented with it report that it engenders about the same level of community we find in an actual hotel. How many friends have you made in hotels? When the person next door is different every day, informal social relationships don't develop easily.

Lots of Experiments, Little Learning

We should know much more about the impact of the work space on knowledge workers, but we don't. There is relatively little concrete knowledge about how to enhance the physical work environments for knowledge workers, even though the past couple of decades have been a period of great ferment as firms experiment with different approaches. "Experiment" is an apt term given firms' lack of knowledge, but the experiments would be even more valuable if they had the other accoutrements of experimentation, including measures, controls, hypotheses, or even the simple recording of lessons learned.

There is little actual measurement of the effects of environment interventions, and very few controlled experiments. Instead, it seems that "fad, fashion, and faith" drive most decisions about new work environments for knowledge workers. The other powerful "f-factor" is finances, which are always given paramount consideration in the form of cost savings. The costs of a given work environment are easy to measure; the benefits are not.

Combining Facilities Changes with
Other Performance Factors

Another reason why there is so little knowledge about what impacts knowledge worker performance is that managers now recognize that the complexity of the work requires a multifaceted approach, which makes individual changes almost impossible to evaluate. New workspace or new technology or new management approaches alone aren't enough to affect productivity. Changes in each of these areas must be closely coordinated to impact performance. In our study of forty-one companies, however, we often found that a new workplace served as the symbolic nucleus of efforts to help knowledge workers perform with greater efficiency, effectiveness, or innovation. Only a few companies were combining a new workspace with other factors, however.

The most compelling new visions, and the most effective implementations, incorporate changes in management and culture, information technology, and the physical workspace. One new vision, for example, comes from the workspace design firm DEGW. It envisions "the city as office" and lays out a variety of metropolitan work locations from which an employee or her organization can choose.

Knowledge workers in such an environment might convene in a collaborative environment where they work with other members of their own organization, or with customers, suppliers, or partners. The setting might be a Starbucks coffee shop (already fast becoming a remote haven for knowledge workers); a hotel lobby; a castle in the mountains; or even a "gentlemen's club" environment, complete with paneled walls, leather couches, and a nip of sherry to lubricate the knowledge transfer process. Where do we sign up for that office?

Workers living in the same area who need connections to data or voice networks could go to an entirely different facility with an entirely different feel, and this facility could also serve multiple organizations. For example, DEGW envisions rentable project space linked to public institutions such as the Tate Museum, or space that is permanently shared among organizations. Royal Dutch Shell's corporate training center in the Netherlands, for example, becomes a Holiday Inn on weekends, which covers much of the cost of the center. In this model, employees' homes are viewed as just another potential work location.

The DEGW model relies heavily on mobile technologies that allow workers to move easily work from one facility to another, and to keep track of where a given worker is at any time. Technology that informs workers within a facility which other workers are there at the time—a face-to-face "buddy list"—would be helpful in bringing about collaboration. It relies on organizational interventions to facilitate collaboration both within and across organizations, and a high degree of coaching and "change management" for workers attempting to maximize their productivity and achieve a satisfactory work-life balance. As a DEGW executive put it:

> Our fastest-growing area is change management, not design. It is taking off like crazy. People are realizing that you can use the physical workplace to instigate business process change.

Many knowledge workers already work across a variety of locations as the DEGW model envisions, but there is relatively little support for their work today. It's sometimes even difficult to connect one's computer to an e-mail or collaboration system while traveling, and relatively few organizations help their employees set up home work environments. The DEGW model could enhance knowledge worker performance by acknowledging the mobility of this type of work, and creating as many friendly, efficient homes for it as possible.

The Need for New Collaborations

Whose job is it to bring about compelling new work environments for knowledge workers? In most organizations, there is insufficient collaboration across HR, IT, and facilities functions—either to create these visions or to make them a reality. A dramatic departure from today's humdrum work environment for knowledge workers would require close collaboration and early involvement from these three support groups. It would also require clear direction from the CEO about the specific needs for knowledge work improvement. This integrated approach is necessary because the new solutions, like DEGW's "city as office," involve all three components, and no single individual can master expertise in the three domains.

Cisco Systems, for example, formed a cross-functional task force to develop an integrated workspace strategy. From the outset, the firm's leadership made it clear they were holding all three functions account-able for the same business goals—cost-effectively improving both em-ployee productivity and satisfaction.

Once Cisco's task force members had identified common goals, they needed a process that would allow the development of a shared understanding of the solutions needed. To start, representatives from each function presented to the group. The facilities unit described how Cisco's knowledge workers were currently using office space. An IT staff member previewed the technologies expected to impact the work-place in the next several years and an HR representative described the envisioned characteristics of Cisco's workforce. Gradually, the task force developed a unified vision of the future work environment the firm needed to create. The group also developed a "shared language" that described what employees do, and, by implication, how they needed to be supported differently. The Cisco task force, for example, got a big boost when the company's own salespeople began asking members to show customers how Cisco was trying to leverage IT and the workspace in its own work environment.

As the need to improve knowledge work environments becomes in-creasingly critical, essential support functions may be combined, or new functions will emerge that combine the strategy and planning as-pects of existing support groups. Some firms have a head start on such capabilities. BT has its Workstyle Consultancy Group and Sun Micro-systems has a Workplace Effectiveness organization that combines as-pects of the HR, IT, and facilities organizations.

Segmentation and Choice—a Model
for Knowledge Workspaces

Although these new visions are appealing, most organizations need a pragmatic approach to making decisions today about knowledge work environments. I can offer a management model that's based on two attributes of knowledge workers that we can assume with some confidence. We know, as I have discussed in previous chapters, that knowledge workers like autonomy (chapter 1 and elsewhere) and are not all alike (chapter 2). My colleagues and I developed a framework (see figure 8-1) that shows the different ways executives can improve the fit between knowledge workers and their physical work environments, the advantages and disadvantages of each approach, and some best practices in choosing and implementing solutions that have the greatest impact on performance. The framework is built on the two key dimensions of knowledge work environments that account for much of the variation we found across the forty-one companies we researched, each of which are reliable attributes of knowledge work. The first dimension is the *degree of segmentation of the group work setting*. Whereas some work settings are highly segmented (i.e., customized for a group of knowl-

FIGURE 8-1

Range of possible work settings solutions

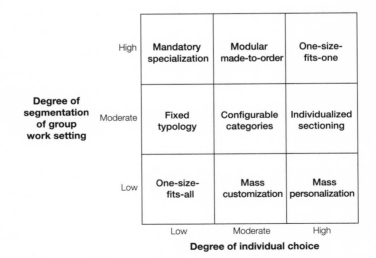

edge workers), others are common to a large number of employees. The second dimension is the *degree of individual choice* granted to knowledge workers to tailor their designated group work setting to meet their individual needs. These can be combined in a matrix to produce a total of nine possible solutions for any given work setting. Below I describe the categories of the dimensions in greater detail and provide examples of companies that fit into each category.

Degree of Segmentation of Work Environments

I've argued throughout this book that knowledge workers vary in their tasks and needs, and it doesn't make sense that they should all get the same physical work environment—even within the same organization. Some of the different segmentation approaches one could use here include the four-cell matrix (introduced in chapter 2) based on judgment and collaboration, the creation/distribution/application distinction, or some other approach that I describe below. For example, transaction workers such as those in call centers need work environments in which they can concentrate on their transactions; integration workers would need an ability to communicate easily with coworkers, and expert workers would need an ability to concentrate. These different knowledge work activities would dictate different work environments.

Segmentation of knowledge worker environments can be undertaken at three basic levels. In general, the greater the degree of segmentation, the greater the degree of fit between worker and work setting, and the greater the number and variety of work settings within an organization.

Low degree of segmentation. Firms with low degrees of segmentation provide one standard work setting for all employees. Employees at SEI Investments, for instance, all work in a large open environment with identical workstations and technologies. For organizations whose workers and work activities are fairly homogenous, such as some architecture or law firms, standardized work settings with low degrees of segmentation may be an easy way of efficiently aligning the work setting with the needs of the majority who work there. Even organizations characterized by a variety of types of workers will implement this approach, however, under certain circumstances. They may use low-segmentation approaches, for example, when they want to contain costs, underscore the move to a nonhierarchical environment, attract and retain a certain type of worker, or encourage a common cultural value, such as open communication, across the organization. This approach is most likely to produce a misfit between the needs of individual knowledge workers and their work environments, however. One manager we spoke with, for example, felt that her firm's move to an open plan environment would substantially compromise the confidentiality required in her job when speaking with clients, and thus inhibit her performance. Some employees or potential employees would vote with their feet, like the SEI recruits who said they couldn't work in a big open room.

Moderate degree of segmentation. Other firms group their employees into a limited number of categories and assign predefined work settings to each. Familiar categorization schemes aimed at identifying appropriate work settings include segmentation of workers by status, geography, or job role. Less familiar, but increasingly popular, categories segment knowledge workers by criteria such as:

- Degree of mobility

- Amount of teamwork versus independent work

- Number of projects undertaken at one time

- Amount and type of communication undertaken with others

Intel, for example, has applied some of these criteria to identify three main types of work environments for three types of knowledge workers: "teamers, nomads, and sitters." This is a segmentation approach for office space purposes, which is different from the IT-oriented segmentation scheme at Intel I described in chapter 2. Such typologies are helpful for organizations whose project types or knowledge workers' needs differ substantially from one another, and they can provide an opportunity to create shared organizational meanings about different types of workers. However, typologies can be difficult to create and implement. What works for one organization may not work as well for another. Merrill Lynch segments its knowledge workers by job role: portfolio managers, traders, and information technology professionals each have their own workspace design and technology solutions. But other organizations may not have enough homogeneity within each job role to segment successfully by role. One telecommunications firm we studied has three very different types of engineers: "parachutists," who drop into projects for a short time to help with a particular issue; "ambassadors," who represent the work of the firm to the outside world; and those who perform heads-down concentrated work on one project at a time.

High degree of segmentation. A few of the organizations we studied have highly segmented group work settings that are specifically tailored to a relatively small number of people on a one-off, group-by-group basis. Instead of assigning the same work setting to all groups of, say, "type A," firms favoring high levels of segmentation create unique solutions for each group. Fidelity Investments, for instance, has external consultants who approach each group independently and analyze work patterns and processes to create a custom-tailored solution specific to that group. Although this type of work setting enables a tighter fit between worker needs and work setting, it can be expensive and time-consuming to implement. Perhaps for this reason, some of the companies we studied that used this approach did so in only part of the firm.

Degree of Individual Choice

Although knowledge workers may provide input into the type of work setting they would like their group to have, most decisions about the designs of group workspaces are made by the organization. In contrast, some solutions offering high degrees of individual choice enable knowledge workers to make decisions about how to configure their own personal work environment within the constraints of a designated group work setting. This appeals, of course, to the desire of knowledge workers to have autonomy at work. Choice is also cheap—at least it doesn't cost anything to let employees bring in their own office accoutrements. Although we found no organizations providing total flexibility to their employees, we did identify three levels of individual choice.

Low degree of choice. Some organizations allow their employees little or no choice in designing their own work environments, which—regardless of their level of segmentation—are fixed and immutable. Employees with low or no individual choice cannot configure their workstations in various ways, nor work at home as they see fit. They may not even be able to bring in their own desk items, as is the case in some hoteling environments. From a technology standpoint, many firms, such as Hewlett-Packard, have developed a common operating environment (COE) that is intended to minimize purchase and support costs. This approach does not guarantee a close fit between a knowledge worker's needs and the work environment, but it is less complex and expensive to manage.

Moderate degree of choice. Just as firms may limit the number of group work settings by establishing a limited, predefined set of solutions, firms may likewise limit an individual's degree of choice by establishing a limited, predefined solution set. A large proportion of our research participants, for example, provide a standard kit of office and technology components or a set of predefined menu options for employees to choose from. Sun Microsystems provides its knowledge workers with a menu of physical work environments (such as private offices, shared team rooms, satellite centers, work from home, etc.) as well as hardware and software options. Other firms offer configurable furniture with options such as adjustable partition heights or furniture on wheels that can be moved around on an as-needed basis. This approach is particularly good for organizations whose workers' needs change often and unpredictably. The hazard is that individuals will choose tools and environments that optimize their own performance instead of the overall organization's. The benefit is likely to be more satisfied workers, which can increase performance and retention.

High degree of choice. A few firms allow their knowledge workers to determine substantial aspects of their own work settings outside of the predefined choices offered by the firm. At some firms, employees are encouraged to bring in and arrange their own furniture, or they are reimbursed for the cost of buying their own technology solutions. Other organizations allow workers to customize their workspaces with decorative items. At Chiat/Day for example, a leading advertising firm that once adopted a radical office design with little choice for personalization, workers can now bring in objects with interesting designs that inspire or amuse them—from surfboards to their own pets. The freedom to customize one's own work environment is perhaps most critical for highly creative workers such as those found at Chiat/Day and IDEO.

How the Dimensions Are Used

Some firms use only one of the nine possible work setting solutions and apply it throughout the firm. IDEO, for example, uses a "mass-personalized" solution in all of its offices. It combines a group work setting low on segmentation (all employees share the same standard group work setting), but high on individual choice (employees are encouraged to bring in their own creative accoutrements to supplement the group solution). Nortel Networks also applies one of the nine solutions—"configurable categories"—throughout the firm. Nortel defines a work setting for each group, but that setting can be further tailored in a modular way by individual employees.

Other firms employ more than one work setting solution. Fidelity Investments, for example, has three solutions in its repertoire. It has rolled out "mandatory specialization" solutions (high segmentation, low choice) and "modular made-to-order" solutions (high segmentation, moderate choice) to about half of its workforce. Yet because of its legacy of "universal planning"—a workplace design trend intended to reduce costs by introducing identical buildings filled with identical cubicles—the remainder of Fidelity's employees still work in a "one-size-fits-all" environment (low segmentation, low choice).

Which solution, or combination of solutions, is best for your organization? The answer will depend in part on the answers to the following questions:

- *How homogenous is your organization?* Organizations whose knowledge workers share common work styles and needs may find that a "one-size-fits-all" solution (low segmentation, low choice) works best. But for organizations whose knowledge workers' needs vary, such a solution may significantly inhibit effectiveness.

- *How important is it for your organization to align knowledge workers' needs and their work settings?* For firms with highly specialized knowledge work, e.g., R&D, managers will want to offer highly segmented solutions with high levels of choice. But other organizations more concerned with enforcing a common value system or work process may prefer to look at "one-size-fits-all" solutions in the lower left quadrant of the matrix.

- *How much control does management want to give knowledge workers in designing their own solutions?* Group work settings can incorporate input from knowledge workers, but experts make the final decision. Only solutions with a high degree of individual choice will allow knowledge workers to tailor their own work-spaces as their needs change.

- *What level of resources are you willing to dedicate?* High degrees of segmentation require greater resources, but can have greater payoffs in enhanced performance. Firms that want to get the biggest bang for their buck may choose to focus on mass-personalized solutions that are less complex and costly yet still give knowledge workers the autonomy and choice they desire.

I believe that for most knowledge workers, the cells of figure 8-1 toward the upper right—high segmentation with high choice—will provide the optimal, if perhaps the most resource-intensive, solution. These work environments provide maximum fit between knowledge worker and work setting, and grant some degree of choice and autonomy.

Only solutions that are carefully implemented, however, will produce the desired fit between knowledge worker and work environment. Solutions are best when developed from the inside out and based on a thorough understanding of work styles and processes. Managers at Nortel Networks spent a year researching work processes across multifunctional teams through interviews and observations to identify the best range of solutions based on the identification of eight different team types. In addition, because all solutions eventually wear out, organizations must monitor the changing needs of their knowledge workers and how new technologies may enable new ways of working. Creating high-performance work environments for an organization's most valuable assets is a matter of constantly refining the options and solutions offered.

Summary

There is no doubt that knowledge workspace decisions will continue to be based on less-than-rigorous criteria, and that cost will remain a very important factor. But there is evidence that the physical workspace impacts knowledge worker performance, and we need to do a better job of housing our most important and expensive personnel. If we could begin to learn from our experiments, it wouldn't take long before we had an impressive base of knowledge to guide future decisions. And applying segmentation and choice is something that managers of knowledge workers can employ today to make their work more productive and effective.

Recommendations for Getting Results from Knowledge Workers

- Despite the rise of virtual technologies, the physical work environment is still a major factor in knowledge workers' performance. More disciplined experiments are necessary to learn the nature of its influence, however.

- Despite this uncertainty, we can say a few things with confidence about knowledge workers and their workplaces, and we should base our interventions on what we know. These facts include, for example, that knowledge workers prefer closed offices, but seem to communicate better in open ones.

- Some degree of segmentation in workplace arrangements for knowledge workers is important.

- Knowledge workers like autonomy, so it's also desirable to give them some degree of choice in how their workplace looks and performs.

- The most compelling new visions, and the most effective implementations, for knowledge workspaces incorporate changes in management and culture, information technology, and the physical workspace. This requires new levels of collaboration across support functions.

Managing Knowledge Workers

How should knowledge workers be managed in order to extract the highest possible level of performance and results? How should a manager or leader act within a knowledge-intensive organization? How does knowledge work management differ from the other, more traditional forms of management? This is a somewhat familiar area, unlike the physical facilities for knowledge work I discussed in the previous chapter; we already know a good deal about how best to manage knowledge work—in part because some of the received wisdom about managing knowledge workers also applies to other types of workers. Some might argue that the attributes of good managers and leaders in general are also the attributes of good managers and leaders of knowledge workers.*

A contrarian might argue, however, that management doesn't even have a role in knowledge work. The idea of "management"—a separate role focused on the planning, oversight, and monitoring of others'

---

*I discussed some of the topics in this chapter with Warren Bennis, and some of the ideas are undoubtedly his. I published parts of the chapter in his Festschrift volume, *The Future of Leadership*, ed. Warren Bennis, Gretchen M. Spreitzer, and Thomas G. Cummings (Jossey-Bass, 2001).

work—was appropriate for the industrial age, but some would suggest that it is no longer necessary in an era of autonomous, self-motivated knowledge workers. Will teams of computer programmers, marketing analysts, researchers, and other knowledge-intensive jobs essentially manage themselves?

I believe there is still an important role, albeit a different one, for management in overseeing knowledge work and workers. In fact, I'd argue that the growth of knowledge work is the single most important factor driving the future of management. Because those who are managed will be a substantially different group from workers of the past, management itself will have to change, in some cases dramatically. But what are the new tasks of management, and how will they be influenced by the importance of knowledge and knowledge work?

I will spend the bulk of this chapter focusing on a set of management attributes that are at the core of knowledge work, and perhaps less relevant to traditional forms of administrative or operational work. I'll also discuss managerial topics—such as external sourcing—that have recently become more relevant to knowledge work. At the end of the chapter, I'll nod in passing to some traditional management concerns that may be well-known capabilities, but take on a somewhat different meaning in the knowledge work context.

A Brief Look at the Traditional Management Virtues

The old model of management was formed to deal with a very different set of circumstances than those organizations face today. Industrial work predominated at the turn of the last century. Many workers knew only craft or home-based labor, and were unfamiliar with working in large organizations. Most were relatively uneducated; many were motivated to work hard only by external pressure. Employees were often in unions; managers were not. Industrial work was not yet very productive, and substantial analysis and redesign was necessary to improve it. The concept of "bureaucracy," formulated by the sociologist Max Weber, was considered a positive attribute involving professionalism, clear divisions of labor, and work roles that were independent of the individual.[1]

While it's been evident for years that this model no longer applies to the contemporary work environment, no clear alternative has come along to take its place. What attributes of the old management model still make sense in the knowledge work era, and which should be dropped? It's worth a quick review of that design for the manager's role in order to assess which of its aspects are still relevant:

- Management was considered a separate role from the rest of work. Managers managed, and workers worked, and there was little overlap between the two sets of activities.

- Management processes assumed that workers did manual work that could be observed by managers. Work started and ended at clear times, and workers' performance was easily measured.

- Workers were assumed to be selfish and out to maximize only their own success; managers supposedly had the good of the broader organization in mind at all times.

- It was believed that a primary activity of first-line and middle managers was to convey information to and from workers, and to represent workers to senior management. Skipping links in the chain of communication was considered disloyal or rabble-rousing.

- Work processes and activities were subject to analysis and improvement, but the activities of managers were not viewed as accessible for assessment or improvement.

- Management was viewed as requiring a higher level of conceptual capabilities and was perceived to be superior to, and more valuable than, nonmanagerial work.

- It was assumed that managers could do workers' jobs better than the workers themselves; indeed, it was part of the manager's responsibility to instruct workers on how to perform their jobs more effectively.

- The manager's job was to think, and the worker's job to do (as Henry Ford put it, "What I want is a good pair of hands, unfortunately I must take them with a person attached!").

New Management Priorities

These generalizations about management, of course, make little sense in an economy and society in which knowledge predominates. Managing with knowledge and managing knowledge work require that most of these assumptions must change. They have already begun to change, as managers of knowledge workers realize their inappropriateness. Again, however, what it means to manage knowledge workers has not been fully articulated. While not all organizations and work settings are knowledge-intensive, in the United States, Japan, and Europe we have reached the point of critical mass of those organizations at which knowledge should drive the way we think about management.

Management thinkers have talked for decades about a new future for management, but its realization awaited the right proportion of knowledge workers and the widespread recognition that knowledge is the firm's most critical asset. The problem has been apparent, but it hasn't been solved. Peter Drucker called it a key aspect of "management's new role" to "make knowledge more productive"—an unobjectionable statement today, though Drucker said it more than thirty years ago—and we still haven't figured out how to do it.[2]

Just as the proliferation of industrial workers created a need for a professional management class, the emergence and maturation of the knowledge worker role is the driver of what management will be in the next century. Because knowledge is an invisible asset that resides largely in the minds of human beings, management can no longer be about close observation and monitoring. Because knowledge work can be and is done by managers as well as workers, strict separations between worker and manager no longer make sense. Because knowledge work has become the key to growth and differentiation in today's economy, the differential in cost and value between knowledge work and management has decreased. Management in the "knowledge economy" is a different game, with different rules.

Given these important background factors, managers in the future will have to adapt their activities to the new world they'll face. In the remainder of this chapter, I'll describe some of the specific changes management may undergo, including:

- From overseeing work to doing it too

- From organizing hierarchies to organizing communities

- From hiring and firing workers to recruiting and retaining them

- From building manual skills to building knowledge skills

- From evaluating visible job performance to assessing invisible knowledge achievements

- From ignoring culture to building a knowledge-friendly culture

- From supporting the bureaucracy to fending it off

- From relying on internal personnel to considering a variety of sources

While each of these attributes of knowledge work management may represent only an evolutionary change from how managers worked in the late twentieth century, in aggregate they comprise a managerial revolution.

Managing and Doing Knowledge Work

Perhaps the most important thing to mention about managers of knowledge work is that they'll do more than just manage. In many cases, the knowledge work manager also performs knowledge work. Managers in law, consulting, and accounting firms often have their own clients. A university administrator may still teach and do research. A manager of investment analysts in a mutual funds firm has his own industry to cover as an analyst. The manager today is what might be called a "player/coach"—doing work, yet overseeing others who do it at the same time.[3]

There are a number of benefits to this hybrid role. Knowledge work managers who do work too can stay in touch with the real concerns of clients and customers. These managers probably enjoy doing nonmanagerial knowledge work, and may feel it necessary to be respected by those they manage. As Rosabeth Kanter puts it, "But now, as hierarchies are deemphasized, the formal authority derived from hierarchy is less important than professional expertise in gaining the respect required for influence and leadership."[4]

But the player/coach role creates conflicts and uncertainties. How much time should be spent doing versus managing doers? Should the manager of knowledge workers be the best knowledge worker in the bunch? If so, should he or she be "wasting" time on managing? And if the manager performs too much actual knowledge work, other traditional managerial functions, such as budgeting, planning, and human resource management, may suffer.

The right balance of managing and doing knowledge work varies, of course, by the particular individual and the situation. Fundamentally, however, managing others is a different role from being an individual contributor. It involves developing others, in addition to cultivating one's own capabilities. Managing is long-term and ambiguous; being an individual contributor typically involves quick results.

Consequently, knowledge work managers often spend more time doing work than managing it. Anyone creating or performing one of these hybrid roles should anticipate that problems will ensue on an ongoing basis.

Building Knowledge Work Communities

Knowledge workers are increasingly described as autonomous free agents. Even though the "free agent nation" rhetoric of the dot-com boom was overblown, there are still many knowledge workers who work independently of any single organization, and their numbers will probably increase over time. But where will these knowledge workers find community? Spending your day working with knowledge doesn't obviate the need for community—not just chat rooms, but real face-to-face contact with other human beings. Knowledge workers don't have labor unions, and they don't want them. Even the role of professional associations is fading in today's cross-functional workplace, as engineers work just as closely with marketers, manufacturers, and financiers as they do with other engineers. And as we all work longer hours, we have increasing difficulty finding community outside of the workplace. MIT professor Tom Malone has proposed that "guilds" of knowledge worker free agents will serve as communities, but there is little evidence of their emergence thus far.[5]

One of the key roles of the knowledge work manager, then, is to create work communities. But on what basis? Work teams may form some degree of community, but just because team members are trying to achieve a common objective doesn't mean they want to share. And in global, virtual organizations, teams are scattered around the world. Perhaps a more viable basis for community is knowledge. Knowledge workers who produce the same types of knowledge may be the most willing to commune.

In fact, knowledge-based communities are at the heart of the recent "communities of practice" movement.[6] The members of a community of practice do similar work, but the purposes of their association are knowledge sharing and social interaction. The members of such communities all generate knowledge, share it, and use it—generally for free. The manager's job then becomes forming these communities, nurturing and facilitating their exchanges of knowledge and social capital, and ensuring that one community overlaps with another when necessary.

Knowledge communities are already well established in many consulting firms, where they are a primary means of connecting geographically dispersed consultants who share an interest in a particular industry, business problem, or technology. Most such groups meet face-to-face as well as electronically. But knowledge communities are also viable in industrial firms. Chrysler, for example, organized over one hundred "Tech Clubs" so that new car engineers in diverse specialty areas could share their learnings with each other. Each club had a facilitator (i.e., a manager of a knowledge community) and an electronic repository for shared knowledge. The clubs were viewed as a means of nurturing shared technical knowledge in an environment where almost all work was on cross-functional platform teams. These teams improved Chrysler's new car development, but they also inhibited detailed knowledge sharing among specialists, and were viewed as a barrier to improved quality; the tech clubs allowed for the flow of knowledge across teams. However, after a merger created Daimler-Chrysler, executives tried to establish tech clubs that crossed the Atlantic and the merged organization, but geographical and cultural barriers proved too strong for the clubs to flourish. It certainly isn't easy to create and nurture community across global organizations, but the most successful knowledge work managers will have to learn how to do it.

Recruiting and Retaining Knowledge Workers

Perhaps the single most important task of the knowledge work manager is recruiting and retaining the best knowledge workers. Interventions after people are hired are critical, of course—that's generally what this book is about—but there's a lot to be said for hiring smart, capable, creative people who can produce from the first day on the job. In my view this factor is the one most frequently encountered in the success of the best knowledge-intensive firms. The Mercks, the Microsofts, and the McKinseys—all highly successful knowledge-intensive firms—of the world put extraordinary efforts into recruiting the smartest and most talented workers in their industries, and at keeping their high performers. With an expected shortage of workers in the next decade, the war for knowledge talent will only become fiercer. There are factors other than raw talent that affect performance—as I hope this book (and some other recent literature) demonstrates.[7] But it's not a bad trait with which to start.

The importance of recruiting and retention is well-known. What is less familiar, however, is the best approach for recruiting and retaining knowledge workers. How, for example, can firms ensure that new recruits have the basic intellectual curiosity that will motivate learning throughout their careers? My own experience as a professor at some prestigious universities suggests that being admitted to and graduating from one of them is not a guarantee of intellectual curiosity. One important indicator may be the degree to which an applicant has attempted to gather knowledge about the company at which he or she seeks employment. If a job applicant hasn't demonstrated high motivation to get the position—consulted a company's Web site or annual report before an interview—it's unlikely that this person will ardently consume knowledge if he or she is hired.

There are other generic knowledge worker traits in addition to intellectual curiosity. The ability to communicate well is one; perhaps more firms should try to elicit actual writing, listening, and speaking capabilities during the recruiting process. Another is the ability to get along well with people. An IT manager I know deliberately induces frustration in potential recruits to his organization by having a secretary inform them that the results of tests they've taken have been delayed. Applicants who are rude to the secretary do not get offered a job.

Recruiting will have to become a high-priority, continuous process for organizations interested in getting the best knowledge worker talent. Instead of beginning to look for a knowledge worker when there's an opening, it will become important to look all the time. Firms should maintain a database of knowledge workers whom they might want to employ at some time. Cisco Systems, the fast-growing maker of Internet equipment, already has a database with the names of sixty-five thousand potential employees. And when someone applies for a job and there's no current opening, Cisco managers keep track of their skills and backgrounds for potential future use. Cisco even attempts to increase the general population's level of skills with IT networks—and further populate its recruiting base—with its Networking Academy.

The problem of finding knowledge workers is acute today, but demographic trends suggest that it will get worse. In the United States, for example, there is expected to be a shortage of 3 million workers between the ages of 25 and 44 to replace the generation of workers above it when they retire.[8] Given the coming shortage of knowledge workers, the effort to retain such workers will be as difficult as that required to recruit them—and of course recruitment and retention policies are related. It will undoubtedly be expensive to retain the best workers, but retention will remain cheaper than having to recruit new ones. It's also heartening that knowledge workers say that money is not the primary factor in retention. In a recent Hay Group survey of workers in over three hundred companies, workers said that the ability to learn new skills was far more important in their willingness to stay with a job than money or any other factor. Pay was the least important factor of fifty surveyed (I must confess that I find this difficult to believe). Workers in the survey also said they valued feedback from supervisors and information about what was going on in the company.

Companies should have well-defined procedures for dealing with the planned departure of a valued knowledge worker. At Cypress Semiconductor, for example, the structured process kicks in when a star employee declares an intention to leave. It begins with a response to the announcement within five minutes, and culminates in a meeting with T. J. Rodgers, Cypress's CEO. Rodgers is a strong believer in the primacy of human assets in the knowledge economy—and has a bulldog-like personality as well. I would not want to announce my departure to him. Cypress also has very highly structured processes for recruiting, and gets some of the best people in the industry.[9]

Unfortunately, the evidence suggests that most firms are moving in the wrong direction on recruitment and retention issues. They are telling their employees that they need to be "career self-reliant," managing their own careers and increasing their employability for a variety of jobs. Then, as Jeffrey Pfeffer puts it, " . . . the companies are then surprised when they face the very turnover that their programs have helped foster."[10] Other research suggests that the common downsizing programs in American businesses only increase turnover, and lower morale for those who do remain.[11] Perhaps the only real answer to this issue is to return, as Pfeffer advocates, to lifetime employment arrangements for talented knowledge workers who want them.

Building and Propagating Knowledge Skills

Managers have always been responsible for helping workers build their skills. At the turn of the last century, Frederick Taylor urged them to invest in workers' abilities to perform manual work. Now, of course, the skills involve knowledge acquisition, analysis, and use. As Ikujiro Nonaka, the Japanese knowledge creation guru, often comments, "the learning organization must be a teaching organization."[12] But what should the learning organization teach? Currently, as I argued in chapter 6, very little energy is focused by either universities or employers on building personal information and knowledge skills—how to search for information and knowledge, how to determine which sources are credible, how to manage personal information and knowledge environments, and so forth. Most knowledge workers underinvest in their own skills and knowledge environments.

Another component of knowledge skill building is encouraging knowledge workers to teach as well as to learn. Managers must encourage knowledge workers to come to understand how they do their own work, and then to teach explicit and tacit knowledge to others. Knowledge workers should be held accountable not only for developing their own skills, but also for ensuring that they are not the only ones who possess them. An organization's knowledge and learning managers should provide some guidelines as to how best to transfer different types of knowledge.

Highly tacit knowledge, for example, is probably best transferred through longer-term, face-to-face mentoring relationships, while explicit knowledge can be codified (written down, for example) and transferred electronically. Of course, it's the tacit stuff that matters at the high end of knowledge work. How do you cultivate an executive presence? How do you develop a nose for important scientific problems? These kinds of learnings can only be communicated through substantial face-to-face interaction.

Creating a Knowledge-Friendly Culture

Managers have not often focused on building cultures, and when they have their approach has often been to reinforce the existing corporate culture. But knowledge work managers need to build company cultures that are in accordance with what knowledge workers want, or they will leave. A manager of knowledge workers quoted in the *Wall Street Journal* commented, "If you're buying intellectual equity, the culture of the company is everything."[13] What are the attributes of a culture that would attract knowledge workers? Drawing from Rosabeth

Kanter and Warren Bennis, the "Five Fs" characterize the most desirable knowledge-oriented culture (perhaps all workers would value most of these traits!): fast, flexible, focused, friendly, and fun.[14] We realized that these attributes were important in the dot-com era, but we may have forgotten about them in the post-boom "Dark Ages" of the past few years, when many knowledge workers have been happy just to have jobs. The Five Fs will undoubtedly come back as labor markets tighten because of an improved economy and demographic shifts.

The pace of business life seems to gain speed continually, and knowledge workers will want their firms' cultures to keep pace. Nothing is more frustrating than a firm that responds slowly to business trends because of bureaucratic inertia. Similarly, the knowledge-oriented firm needs to be flexible—changing business models with the competitive environment. Knowledge workers want their firms to be focused on the business issues that matter to their firms' success. And because life is short and work is long, knowledge workers want their jobs to be friendly and fun.

The knowledge worker culture is also one of community. Managers must work jointly with workers to create a communal sense of purpose and vision. Knowledge workers don't want to work toward a goal because someone else has set it, but rather because they believe that it's right.

Specific knowledge-oriented behaviors must also be an integral part of the culture. It should be perfectly acceptable, for example, to sit at one's desk and read a business-relevant book—normally, in the United States at least, a knowledge behavior that's restricted to personal time. The culture should also support decision making and action based on knowledge and facts, not gut feel and intuition alone. Managers of knowledge workers must set examples with their own decisions.

Fending Off Bureaucracy

Most knowledge workers have a justifiable antipathy toward bureaucracy. They would like to be able to do their work without excessive rules, policies, or formal processes. Many organizations, however, strive to control knowledge workers by implementing these very strictures. Therefore, managers of knowledge workers need to fend off the bureaucracy whenever possible, or at least provide a buffer between it and the knowledge workers. As Warren Bennis and Pat Biederman found out in a study of "great groups" of knowledge workers, including Xerox PARC researchers, Lockheed's Skunk Works, and Manhattan Project scientists, most such initiatives included managers who played the role of bureaucratic intermediary.[15] They kept high-achieving knowledge workers happy and productive by removing barriers and giving the bureaucracy what it required with minimal bother.

However, since managers of knowledge workers are themselves knowledge workers, many of them will not find this an interesting way to spend time. In fact, the need to serve as a bureaucracy-buster may make it difficult to recruit knowledge workers to become managers. One potential solution in large groups of knowledge workers is to employ an effective intermediary between knowledge workers and the bureaucracy, who is not him- or herself a knowledge creator. Another solution is to make the bureaucratic role a temporary one that's held on a rotational basis, as universities have long done with department chairpeople.

Sourcing of Knowledge Work

The responsible, opportunity-minded knowledge work executive considers alternative sourcing of knowledge work before building an internal resource. While the external sourcing of knowledge workers has long been established in certain domains (strategy consulting and legal services, for example), there are some relatively new options that executives must consider with due diligence, the following among them.

Contracting for external expertise. When the needed knowledge isn't firm-specific and when there are external sources available, it may make sense to contract for knowledge rather than to hire or develop it internally. This is a familiar approach, but managers may not be aware of the best circumstances under which to do it.[16] Contractors can be long- or short-term, individual knowledge workers or firms, and based on process (e.g., payments for time and materials) or outputs (payments for completed products or services). Some organizations even contract with former employees, which can be a means of avoiding lost knowledge due to retirement.[17] With contracting, however, the final responsibility for performing a knowledge work process typically remains within a company.

Outsourcing. With outsourcing, the responsibility for performing the service is turned over to an external organization. The first knowledge-intensive process to be widely outsourced was information technology, including applications development (clearly a knowledge work activity) in many contracts. But other processes are increasingly being outsourced as well. Thus far most business process outsourcing (BPO) projects have been for transactional services, rather than knowledge work processes. However, BPO vendors do offer knowledge-intensive services for a variety of business functions, including such offerings as supply chain optimization, financial analysis, human resource planning, and market planning and segmentation. Some organizations are already beginning to outsource these analytically oriented functions.

Offshoring. An increasingly popular sourcing decision is to go "offshore" with business processes, either by outsourcing to offshore service providers, or hiring offshore employees. Again, the first work to be taken offshore was administrative in nature—data entry, back-office processing, and low-level programming—and the primary objective was to lower costs. Now, however, it is clear that organizations can take the most knowledge-intensive activities offshore, and their objectives include taking advantage of the knowledge worker talent available in offshore labor markets. Microsoft has moved not only low-level programming to India, but high-level architecture and design activities. General Electric started its move to India with lower-level services, but has since established the John F. Welch Technology Centre (JWFTC) outside Bangalore, and employs this facility for research and product development activities in many of its diverse businesses. GE Capital, for example, first went to India for back-office processing, but now uses statistical experts at the JWFTC to develop new algorithms for automated loan decision making. No matter how sophisticated the expertise involved, it's likely that it can be found outside of the traditional Western markets.

Open sourcing. Noticing the power of the "open source" model of product development in the software industry, organizations are beginning to apply the model to a variety of knowledge work activities. There are many more smart people outside of any firm than there are within it. Eli Lilly is one of the most aggressive adopters of this model in the pharmaceutical industry. Its subsidiary InnoCentive offers online problems in biology and chemistry for solution by a worldwide scientific community. Lilly makes the network available not only to solve its own scientific problems, but also those of other participating firms, including DuPont and Boeing. Scientists can be paid tens of thousands of dollars for solving these problems. Lilly or the other solution-seeking firms pay only if their problem is solved—a completely different model from the typical employee-based arrangement in which employees get paid regardless of whether they solve a problem. No doubt more such "open innovation" business models will emerge.

The Difficulty of Finding and Keeping Knowledge Work Managers

It may be much easier to source a good knowledge worker than a good knowledge work manager. The role conflicts involved in doing and managing knowledge work, the need to balance creativity and autonomy with bureaucracy, and the difficulties of herding knowledge worker "cats" can make this a frustrating and difficult job. And knowledge workers know it. For many, the power, prestige, and increased income that often accompany managerial roles are not worth the trade-offs.

Within the literature on the management of innovation and R&D, it's a common idea to advocate dual tracks for career advancement. Those with potential as managers go into a managerial track, and those with no management orientation can move up to become "Fellows" or "Distinguished Engineers." Given the differences between knowledge work management and the traditional type, however, it may make sense to have a particular track devoted to cultivating knowledge workers who can become knowledge work managers or player/coaches.

Perhaps we can also look to universities for some help in solving the problem of filling such jobs. "Player/coach" roles are common there, for example. College presidents and deans often get tenured professorial appointments, so they can retreat from the pressures of knowledge work management when they burn out. As I mentioned above, department chair positions are often rotational; each senior faculty member with any administrative talent whatsoever (unfortunately, this rarely includes all professors in the department) is expected to take a turn. Perhaps we'll see more temporary or rotational knowledge work managers over time.

Good Managerial Hygiene in the Knowledge Age

I will now discuss the list of managerial traits that apply to all kinds of workers and organizations, but are also important to mention in the context of knowledge work, and require a particular slant when viewed in that context. None of these should be a surprise, although the knowledge work angle may be new to some readers.

Putting the organization in context. Knowledge workers within large organizations are even less content than other types of workers to be "mushrooms," kept in the dark and fed manure. They need to know the broader context in which they work: the industry direction, the company's positioning within the industry, key corporate initiatives, specific performance goals, and how the individual's performance relates to those factors. It's usually first-line managers who supply this context and translate it into terms that are meaningful to each individual.

Aligning projects with corporate direction. Knowledge workers need to work on projects that they personally find interesting and meaningful, and they also need to contribute to the goals of their organizations. It's usually the knowledge worker's manager who reconciles these potentially conflicting objectives. We've all heard of the 15 percent personal time allowance for researchers at 3M, but even there, 85 percent of researchers' time must be agreed upon with the knowledge worker's manager. When I managed a group of researchers, this was one of the most difficult ongoing tasks I performed.

Brokering and learning from dissent. All workers should be allowed to express dissent and constructively criticize their organizations, but this is particularly important for knowledge workers. First, they're very capable of informed dissent. Second, if they can't dissent they are likely to feel stifled and unappreciated. It's the manager's job to ensure that the criticism is constructive, and that the organization learns from its internal critics. As an example, the president of Babson College once announced an unplanned holiday for students. About twenty faculty protested via e-mail, arguing that they had insufficient warning to deal with the change. The president wisely canceled the holiday (before it had been officially announced to students), which showed that he was listening to his faculty and was able to learn from opposing views.

Redesigning and improving knowledge work. One of the functions of management has always been to try to improve the performance of work. In the Industrial Age, this took the form of Frederick Taylor's time-and-motion studies. But if today's work is knowledge work, the work improvement function must address the largely invisible steps in knowledge work production. I've described the process perspective on knowledge work in chapter 4, but it's the job of the manager to oversee this type of change—in a participative fashion, of course.

Orchestrating group decisions. Most workers would like to participate in decisions about where a business function or unit is going, but it's particularly important for knowledge workers. They are paid for their ability to think, make decisions, and take informed actions—so why not involve them in key decisions? Just as knowledge workers want to participate in the design of their work, they also want to be involved in the decisions that affect them. Therefore, the manager of knowledge workers needs to create highly participative decision-making processes— no autocrats need apply.

Harnessing good intent. It's been said of most workers that they want to do a good job, and I think it's even more true of knowledge workers. In their case, "doing a good job" means staying busy, being intellectually engaged in their work, feeling that their work has a positive impact, and getting feedback on how their work is going. Managers who can harness that good intent will usually find that they are getting well over forty hours per week of thinking, communicating, and solving problems from their knowledge workers.

Enabling boundary-spanning. Cutting across organizational boundaries, both inside and outside specific organizations, is a useful approach to spreading innovations, best practices, and lessons learned. Knowledge workers are particularly oriented to this activity because of their intellectual curiosity and their desire to learn. Managers should give knowledge workers many opportunities to cross organizational boundaries, including participating in rotational programs, visiting customers, attending industry conferences, working with universities, and so forth. I generally believe (and there is some research suggesting) that the more knowledge organizations give to the outside world, the more they get in return.

Facilitating social networks. I wrote about these networks for knowledge workers in chapter 7, but I didn't discuss there the role of the manager in facilitating such networks. It's the manager who needs to decide which groups of people in the organization need to be collaborating and communicating with which other groups. This sort of decision would logically lead to a set of programs and interactions designed to build ties across groups and individuals. For example, an executive at Hewlett-Packard concluded in the 1980s that its joint venture in Japan, Yokogawa Hewlett-Packard (YHP), had some approaches to manufacturing quality that could improve quality in the rest of the company. So they embarked upon a series of visits—Japanese managers to the United States, U.S. managers to Japan—that would build those social networks. The collaborations had the desired effect, and many of YHP's approaches were adopted worldwide. This never would have happened if the face-to-face contacts hadn't been initiated.[18]

Summary

In this chapter I've described how to think about the management and leadership of knowledge workers. Some aspects of management as it is currently understood and practiced will persist with this category of work; others are largely new.

As knowledge work becomes the primary work of the organization, management and managers will continue to exist, but not necessarily in recognizable form. The old model of the manager who sits in an office staring down at toiling workers, only occasionally making a visit to the factory floor, is now officially obsolete. The new managers appear suspiciously like knowledge workes, but perform more than day-to-day knowledge work. They also source and recruit knowledge workers, create for them a positive and communal work environment, and remove obstacles to their creative and productive activity. They may not be the smartest knowledge workers on the team, but should be the savviest about how to motivate and reward colleagues. Rather than sitting at the top of the hierarchy, the new managers must subsume their own egos to those of the knowledge workers they manage.

Of course, if we're going to create any precision about which management approaches work best with which types of work and workers, we're going to have to begin measuring and learning from experiments in the domain of management—with technology, the physical workspace, and other factors that influence knowledge work performance. Though we may want to vary only one factor at a time to make it possible to measure each intervention, the fact is that these different factors travel in pairs and triplets. While I have treated each factor separately in its own chapter, the manager of knowledge workers has to think about these factors as they work together. For example, if you were going to shift toward a model of knowledge workers in self-governing teams from a management standpoint, you might well support those teams with new collaboration technologies, the ability to share documents across individual knowledge workers, and a physical workspace that lets team members sit close to each other for greater ease in informal communications.

The problem, of course, is that we don't typically have managers who understand all of these performance-related factors and how they interact with each other in the real world. Managers and leaders of organizations try out snippets of factors to try to improve perfor-mance—a new search tool here, a new office chair there. However, there is no holistic program to try to understand how knowledge workers can be made—or at least facilitated—to perform more pro-ductively and effectively. If knowledge worker performance is one of our most pressing economic issues, surely managers can begin to un-derstand and act on the factors that affect their performance.

Now that you have read this entire book—or have come here to peek at how it ends—you may wonder what happens if we do nothing. What consequences will ensue if we don't make some successful efforts at improving knowledge worker performance? The consequences are fairly dire. Organizations that don't address these issues will fall behind their competitors that do, because knowledge work is at the center of many organizations today, and it is the type of activity that most drives growth. Knowledge-intensive industries that don't improve how knowledge workers do their work won't produce better products and services for their customers, and will eventually go out of business. Countries whose knowledge workers aren't highly productive will lose jobs to other parts of the world where knowledge workers are paid less and produce more for the money. Peter Drucker wasn't exaggerating when he noted that the fate of advanced economies depends on mak-ing knowledge workers more productive. There is no business or eco-nomic issue that is more important to our long-term competitiveness and standard of living.

Recommendations for Getting Results from Knowledge Workers

- Effective management can be extremely important for get-ting the best out of knowledge workers, ensuring that they have a productive work environment, and keeping them happy within their organizations.

- Managers of knowledge workers often have to be knowledge workers themselves; they are "player/coaches." Getting the right balance of playing and coaching is important, but it is very difficult.

- Knowledge workers work in communities, so the knowledge work manager must be skilled at helping to create and nurture community, even when it needs to operate across great geographical distances.

- Since hiring and retaining good knowledge workers is a critical activity, their managers should have well-developed processes for identifying and bringing in the best possible people, and for convincing them to stay when they threaten to wander.

- Effective managers of knowledge work need to create knowledge-friendly cultures, and to fend off the bureaucracy so that their workers are not overly burdened by it.

- While initial examples of outsourcing were primarily transactional in nature, more sophisticated knowledge work is increasingly being outsourced, taken offshore, or managed as an "open source" capability. In order to compete, organizations need sourcing strategies for the key knowledge work they employ.

Notes

Chapter 1

1. James W. Cortada, "Where Did Knowledge Workers Come From?" in *Rise of the Knowledge Worker*, ed. James W. Cortada (Boston: Butterworth-Heinemann, 1998), 3–21.

2. Fritz Machlup, *The Production and Distribution of Knowledge in the United States* (Princeton, NJ: Princeton University Press, 1958; republished 1992).

3. James Brian Quinn, *Intelligent Enterprise: A Knowledge and Service Based Paradigm for Industry* (New York: Free Press, 1992).

4. I have written about processes in *Process Innovation: Reengineering Work through Information Technology* (Boston: Harvard Business School Press, 1993); and *Mission Critical: Realizing the Promise of Enterprise Systems* (Boston: Harvard Business School Press, 2000).

5. I wrote about knowledge management in *Working Knowledge* (with Laurence Prusak) (Boston: Harvard Business School Press, 1997); and in *The Attention Economy: Understanding the New Currency of Business* (with John C. Beck) (Boston: Harvard Business School Press, 2001).

6. John Seely Brown and Paul Duguid, *The Social Life of Information* (Boston: Harvard Business School Press, 2000), 95.

7. Julian E. Orr, *Talking About Machines: An Ethnography of a Modern Job* (Ithaca, NY: Institute for Research on Learning Press, 1996), 1.

8. W. Chan Kim and Renée Mauborgne, "Fair Process: Managing in the Knowledge Economy," *Harvard Business Review* (January 2003): 127–136.

9. Warren Bennis, *Managing People Is Like Herding Cats: Warren Bennis on Leadership* (Provo, UT: Executive Excellence Publishing, 1999).

10. T. S. Eliot, *Old Possum's Book of Practical Cats* (1939; illustrated ed., New York: Harcourt, 1982).

Chapter 2

1. An earlier version of this matrix was developed by Leigh Donoghue and Jeanne Harris of Accenture to describe different strategies for knowledge management. See

"Knowledge Management Strategies that Create Value," *Outlook* (then a publication of Andersen Consulting), January 1999, 1. Online at http://www.accenture.com/xd/ xd.asp?it=enweb&xd=ideas\outlook\1.99\over_currente4.xml.

2. This example taken from Dorothy Leonard-Barton, *Wellsprings of Knowledge* (Boston: Harvard Business School Press, 1995).

3. Several of these process attributes were suggested to me by Ranganath Nayak.

4. Thomas H. Davenport and Nitin Nohria, "Case Management and the Integration of Labor," *Sloan Management Review* (Winter 1994): 11–23.

5. Don Cohen and Laurence Prusak, *In Good Company: How Social Capital Makes Organizations Work* (Boston: Harvard Business School Press, 2001).

Chapter 3

1. Peter Drucker quoted in Brent Schlender, "Peter Drucker Sets Us Straight," *Fortune*, December 29, 2003. On the Web at http://www.fortune.com/fortune/investing/ articles/0,15114,565912,00.html.

2. Peter F. Drucker, "The New Productivity Challenge," *Harvard Business Review* (November–December 1991): 70.

3. If I seem a bit defensive about this, it's because Michael Skapiner of the *Financial Times* suggested this Taylorist connection in a column reviewing an article I'd written. See his "Ignorant on Knowledge," *Financial Times*, November 13, 2002, 16.

4. Charles Leadbeater, *Living on Thin Air: The New Economy* (New York: Viking Press, 1999).

5. For an example of how to assess self-reported attention allocation, see Thomas H. Davenport and John C. Beck, *The Attention Economy* (Boston: Harvard Business School Press, 2002).

6. Software Engineering Institute, *The Capability Maturity Model: Guidelines for Improving the Software Process* (Reading: Addison-Wesley, 1995).

7. Mary Beth Crissis, Mike Conrad, and Sandy Shrum, *CMMI: Guidelines for Process Integration and Product Improvement* (Boston: Addison-Wesley, 2003).

8. Teresa Amabile, Constance N. Hadley, and Steven J. Kramer. "Creativity Under the Gun," *Harvard Business Review* (August 2002): 52–61.

9. For a description of recent thinking on corporate experimentation—particularly with regard to new product development processes—see Stefan M. Thomke, *Experimentation Matters* (Boston: Harvard Business School Press, 2003); and Vijay Govindarajan and Chris Trimble, "Strategic Innovation and the Science of Learning," *Sloan Management Review* (Winter 2004): 67–75.

Chapter 4

1. Nelson P. Repenning and John Sterman, "Nobody Ever Gets Credit for Fixing Problems that Never Happened: Creating and Sustaining Process Improvement," *California Management Review* 43, no. 4 (Summer 2001): 64–88.

2. Neil Swidey, "The Revolutionary," *Boston Globe Sunday Magazine*, January 4, 2004.

3. I first employed this distinction in an article with Sirkka Jarvenpaa and Michael Beers, "Improving Knowledge Work Processes," *Sloan Management Review* (Summer 1996): 53–65.

4. Maurice F. Holmes and R. B. Campbell Jr., "Product Development Processes: Three Vectors of Improvement," working paper, MIT Center for Innovation in Product Development, 2003. Available online at https://dspace.mit.edu/handle/1721.1/3819.

5. For one example of the relationship between knowledge sharing and performance, see Jonathon N. Cummings, "Work Groups, Structural Diversity, and Knowledge Sharing in a Global Organization," *Management Science* (50:3, 2004): 352–364.

6. Thomas H. Davenport, Robert I. Thomas, Kevin C. Desouza, "Reusing Intellectual Assets," *Industrial Management*, May 1, 2003, 12–17.

7. John Seely Brown and Paul Duguid, "Organizational Learning and Communities-of-Practice: Toward a Unified View of Working, Learning, and Innovation," *Organization Science* 2 (February 1991): 40–57.

8. Brown and Duguid have elaborated on the process-practice distinction in chapter 4 of *The Social Life of Information* (Boston: Harvard Business School Press, 2000), 91–116.

9. Quote from http://www.ey.com/global/content.nsf/Middle_East/Knowledge_ Management_-_Tools. The Powerpacks as used in the United States are described in a 1997 *Fast Company* article by Mark Fischetti, "PowerPack Man: Dick Loehr's PowerPacks" at http://www.fastcompany.com/magazine/10/powerpack.html.

10. Martin Fowler, "The New Methodology," on http://www.martinfowler.com/articles/newMethodology.html#N400058.

Chapter 5

1. I believe it was Jeanne Harris, my former colleague at Accenture, who first employed a version of this matrix of technologies, though I have modified it from previous versions.

2. See, for example, Anthony Gorry and Michael S. Scott Morton, "A Framework for Management Information Systems," *Sloan Management Review* 13 (1971): 55–70.

3. There are more than a hundred books on knowledge management, but I am partial to Thomas H. Davenport and Laurence Prusak, *Working Knowledge: How Organizations Manage What They Know* (Boston: Harvard Business School Press, 1997).

4. See the case study by Robert G. Eccles and Julie Gladstone, "KPMG Peat Marwick: The Shadow Partner," Harvard Business School case 9-492-002, 1991.

5. 2002 Delphi study by Humboldt University in Berlin.

6. The Partners system and approach is described in greater detail in Thomas H. Davenport and John Glaser, "Just-in-Time Delivery Comes to Knowledge Management," *Harvard Business Review* (July 2002): 107–111.

7. Gloria Gery, *Electronic Performance Support Systems* (Cambridge, MA: Ziff Institute, 1991).

8. For a print-based example of some potential business benefits from blogging, see a fictional case study by Halley Suitt, "A Blogger in their Midst," *Harvard Business Review* (September 2003): 30–40.

Chapter 6

1. See two books by Watts Humphrey, *Introduction to the Personal Software Process* (Boston: Addison-Wesley, 1996); and *Introduction to the Team Software Process* (Boston: Addison-Wesley, 1999).

2. See, for example, Michael Doyle and David Straus, *How to Make Meetings Work!: The New Interaction Method* (New York: Berkley Books, 1993).

3. In addition to me, the researchers on the project included Meredith Vey of Accenture (who did all of the statistical analysis of the user survey), Carla O'Dell of the American Productivity and Quality Center, Mary Lee Kennedy and Susan Conway of Microsoft, and Dan Holtshouse of Xerox.

4. This underinvestment phenomenon has also been suggested by the authors of one of the only texts I know of on the subject of personal information management. See Gordon B. Davis and J. David Naumann, *Personal Productivity with Information Technology* (New York: McGraw-Hill/Irwin, 1997).

5. All results cited in the differences between demographic groups are statistically significant at the .05 level or better unless otherwise noted.

6. See David Allen, *Getting Things Done: The Art of Stress-Free Productivity* (New York: Penguin, 2003).

7. Kevin Lynn of California is such a coach. See http://www.officecoach.com.

Chapter 7

1. Rob Cross and Andrew Parker have written an understandable guide to the social networking analysis used in this chapter. See *The Hidden Power of Social Networks* (Boston: Harvard Business School Press, 2004). Portions of this chapter appeared in an article with Rob Cross and Susan Cantrell called "The Social Side of Performance," *Sloan Management Review* (Fall 2003): 20–22.

2. For detailed descriptions of how to perform social network analysis, see Stanley Wasserman and Katherine Faust, *Social Network Analysis: Methods and Applications*. (New York: Oxford University Press, 1994); and John Scott, *Social Network Analysis: A Handbook* (London: Sage Publications, 1991).

3. Robert Kelley, *How to be a Star at Work: 9 Breakthrough Strategies You Need to Succeed*. (New York: Times Books, 1998).

4. See, for example, see Sharon McKinnon and William Bruns, *The Information Mosaic* (Boston: Harvard Business School Press, 1992).

5. After-Action Reviews are described as used in the U.S. Army by David A. Garvin, *Learning in Action: Putting Organizational Learning to Work* (Boston: Harvard Business School Press, 2003).

6. The HP Connex system is described in Thomas H. Davenport and Laurence Prusak, *Working Knowledge: How Organizations Manage What They Know* (Boston: Harvard Business School Press, 1998), 124.

7. Interface Software press release, "Corporate Social Networking Fuels Growth and ROI for Interface Software Customers," March 8, 2004.

Chapter 8

1. Dave De Long was also involved in the early phases of the study. Aspects of it were described in Thomas H. Davenport, Robert J. Thomas, and Susan Cantrell, "The Art and Science of Knowledge Worker Productivity," *Sloan Management Review* (Fall 2002): 23–30.

2. Frank Becker and William Sims, *Offices that Work: Balancing Cost, Flexibility, and Communication*, Cornell University International Workplace Studies Program, October 2001. Available online at http://iwsp.human.cornell.edu/pubs/pdf/IWS_0002.PDF.

3. Richard Florida, *The Rise of the Creative Class* (Basic Books, 2002), and "The Economic Geography of Talent (working paper, available online at http://www .creativeclass.org/acrobat/AAAG.pdf.

4. M. Lynne Markus, "IT Support for Global Collaboration," Information Work Productivity Council Research Report, January 2004. Available online at http://iwpc.sharepoint.bcentral.com/iwforum/Document%20Library/1/IWPC% 20Research%20-%20IT%20Support%20for%20Global%20Collaboration.mht.

5. McCue (1978) found 20 percent of programming work was solo; Zelkowitz, Shaw, and Gannon (1979) found 20 percent was individual coding; Brill (2000) found 64 percent quiet work. All cited in Becker and Sims, *Offices that Work*.

6. For a discussion of the role of physical facilities in building and maintaining social capital, see chapter 7 in Don Cohen and Laurence Prusak, *In Good Company: How Social Capital Makes Organizations Work* (Boston: Harvard Business School Press, 2001), 155–182.

7. Thomas J. Allen, *Managing the Flow of Technology* (Cambridge, MA: MIT Press, 1984).

8. For the Steelcase approach to measurement, see "Measuring Business Results: The Role of the Workplace," online at http://www.steelcase.com/na/knowledgedesign .aspx?f=10255&c=10907.

Chapter 9

1. Max Weber, *Economy and Society*, ed. G. Roth and C. Wittich (New York: Bedminster Press, 1968).

2. Peter F. Drucker, "Management's New Role," *Harvard Business Review* (November–December 1969): 49–54.

3. One book calls the role the "player manager." See Philip Augar and Joy Palmer: *Player Manager: The Rise of Professionals Who Manage While They Work* (Texere, 2003).

4. Rosabeth Moss Kanter, "Restoring People to the Heart of the Organization," in *The Organization of the Future*, ed. Frances Hesselbein, Marshall Goldsmith, and Richard Beckhard (San Francisco: Jossey Bass, 1997), 139–150.

5. Thomas W. Malone, *The Future of Work* (Boston: Harvard Business School Press, 2004).

6. Etienne Wenger, *Communities of Practice: Learning, Meaning, and Identity* (New York: Cambridge University Press, 1998).

7. For more on the perils of hiring on talent alone, see Boris Groysberg, Ashish Nanda, and Nitin Nohria, "The Risky Business of Hiring Stars," *Harvard Business Review* (May 2004): 92–100; and Thomas J. DeLong and Vineeta Vijayaraghavan "Let's Hear It for B Players," *Harvard Business Review* (June 2003): 96–102.

8. For a discussion of how this shortage relates to the loss of knowledge in the workforce, see David W. DeLong, *Lost Knowledge: Confronting the Threat of an Aging Workforce* (New York: Oxford University Press, 2004).

9. Charles O'Reilly, "Cypress Semiconductor (A): Vision, Values, and Killer Software," Stanford Business School Case Study, Case HR-8A, 1998.

10. Jeffrey Pfeffer, *The Human Equation* (Boston: Harvard Business School Press, 1998), 163.

11. American Management Association, "Corporate Job Creation, Elimination, and Downsizing: Summary of Key Findings," 1997.

12. Ikujiro Nonaka, personal conversation with author, May 9, 2003.

13. Quotation from Tom McHale of Aurora Enterprise Solutions in Thomas Petzinger Jr., "New Business Leaders Find Greater Profit Mixing Work, Caring" *The Wall Street Journal*, 2 April 1999, B1.

14. The Five Fs are attributed to Rosabeth Kanter (for example, in Charles Handy, *The Age of Paradox* [Boston: Harvard Business School Press, 1994]), but I have heard Warren Bennis enumerate them as well.

15. Warren Bennis and Pat Biederman, *Organizing Genius* (Reading: Addison-Wesley, 1997).

16. A discussion of the circumstances under which one might contract for knowledge work is in Alison Davis-Blake and Pamsy P. Hui, "Contracting Talent for Knowledge-Based Competition," in *Managing Knowledge for Sustained Competitive Advantage*, ed. Susan E. Jackson, Michael A. Hitt, and Angelo S. Denisi (Boston: Jossey-Bass, 2003), 178–206.

17. David De Long, *Lost Knowledge: Confronting the Threat of an Aging Workforce.* (New York: Oxford, 2004).

18. For a discussion of the history of quality at HP, see Robert E. Cole, *Managing Quality Fads: How American Business Learned to Play the Quality Game* (New York: Oxford University Press, 1999).

Index

About the Author

TOM DAVENPORT holds the President's Chair in Information Technology and Management at Babson College, and is an Accenture Fellow. At Babson he is also Director of Research at the School of Executive Education and leads three sponsored research programs there on knowledge management, process management, and innovation.

Tom has written, co-authored, or edited ten other books, including the first books on business process reengineering and achieving value from enterprise systems, and the bestseller *Working Knowledge* (with Larry Prusak) on knowledge management. He has written more than one hundred articles for such publications as *Harvard Business Review, Sloan Management Review, California Management Review,* the *Financial Times,* and many other publications. Tom has also been a columnist for *CIO, InformationWeek,* and *Darwin* magazines. In 2003 he was named one of the world's "Top 25 Consultants" by *Consulting* magazine.